ACCEPT. ADAPT. ACT

Building Hope and Resilience in the Wake of a Pandemic

Dr. Mary Thamari & George Ogalo (Editors)

Light-Up Consulting

Copyright © 2020 Light-up Consulting

All rights reserved

Email: *lightup2060@gmail.com*

Contents

FOREWORD 5

ENDORSEMENTS 9

INTRODUCTION 11

LIST OF CONTRIBUTORS 15

PART 1: ACCEPT...17

Stripped of our Illusions, What a Mercy 17

Living Purposefully in the Light of Finitude 26

Change is here: Expect and Embrace it................36

Technology is Thrilling but Humanity will Always be First.42

Red Scarlet: Embracing Psychosocial Support 50

PART 2: ADAPT..57

Adapting Wholeheartedly 57

Enhancing Children's Resilience 65

Parenting: Fun, Faith & Fortitude.....................79

Restoring Family to the Core of Community...........85

How to Stop the Anxiety Pandemic.....................91

The Silence Is Broken: Embracing Hope..............97

MEN @ HOME: ... Courage, Care & Comradeship.............102

PART 3: ACT WITH HOPE 108

The Journey Within: Taking action for Mental Health........108

Opportunity in Crisis 122

Servant Leadership in Stormy Seasons...............129

Reimagining a Post-COVID-19 Future: 134

People, Power, and the Pandemic 148

Leading Organizational Change........................160

Post-COVID Dreams: ... Social-Economic Justice.................172

Reaffirming our Hope In God 184

FOREWORD

Writing about a fast-evolving reality, as COVID-19 has proven to be, is no mean task. It takes the kind of teamwork and collaboration demonstrated by the professionally diverse team of contributors brought together by Dr. Mary Thamari and George Ogalo. It has been my pleasure to be acquainted with the editors in different contexts, especially as one who shares in the vision of the important work they are doing through the organizations they lead; Mary at Life in Abundance and George at FOCUS Kenya. Without doubt, Accept, Adapt, Act is a timely contribution to the pool of resources needed to help the country transition from the inertia generated by the pandemic trauma, to a thriving posture, in spite of its undeniable ravages. By the time this book goes to print, the world will have experienced the painful loss of over half a million lives, with more than 13 million infected cases, and still counting.1 Besides this, the disruption of the global economy, health-care systems, education, social life and livelihoods, confronts us with an existential challenge that has huge implications which Kenya and the rest of the world will continue to grapple with for many years to come.

Although the world has experienced various pandemics in history, the last one a century ago, the impact of COVID-19 is unprecedented, especially in its potential for far-reaching disruption of the global society. Unlike some of the historical pandemics, the spread of Coronavirus

[1] Online. https://www.worldometers.info/coronavirus/. Accessed on 5/7/2020, at 20:27 GMT.

and the devastation it has wrecked in six months has been amplified by technologically enhanced ease of travel and trans-continental human connectivity. Cognizant of this, the book seeks not only to define the reality on personal, organizational and humanitarian fronts, but also provides an interdisciplinary framework and tool for building hope and resilience. Hence, writing this foreword is such a great privilege for me. In a humble way, I share in bringing to you a timely, pioneering Christian initiative of responding to COVID-19 crisis, underlain by a belief in the redemptive mission of God. I recognize there have been various other initiatives to provide perspective, technical expert analysis, opinion and projections as to how COVID-19 impacts on life and livelihoods now and in the near future. Indeed, the leading global institutions like the WHO,2 the IMF3 and World Bank,4 have been at the vanguard of the effort to mitigate against the impacts of the pandemic and have published regular articles and features on the epidemiological, economic and developmental fronts. In our local context as various authors acknowledge in the book, the government, has put in place a raft of measures both of practical interventions as well as civic education to contain the pandemic. For the purposes of this book, it is notable that among others, John Piper's recent Coronavirus and Christ provides a worthy Christian contribution to the ongoing perspective-shaping conversations within the church and beyond. That being said, Accept, Adapt, Act is a work in a class of its own, in at least three ways that I can highlight here.

---

[2] Online. https://www.who.int/emergencies/diseases/novel-coronavirus-2019. Accessed on 5/7/2020
[3] Online. https://www.imf.org/en/Topics/imf-and-covid19. Accessed on 5/7/2020
[4] Online. https://www.worldbank.org/en/who-we-are/news/coronavirus-covid19. Accessed on 5/7/2020

First, it brings together a diverse, inter-disciplinary team of thought leaders and practitioners in their fields, who all take seriously the dynamic interplay of God's sovereignty and human responsibility. As you will find in the book, this foundational commitment is the critical point of departure from the common run of popular approaches and interventions. Second, the authors have endeavored to blend social research with great sensitivity to the local context and its emergent public health concerns and social justice issues, which have been brought to light by the onslaught of COVID-19. Third, as the three-pronged structure of the book reveals, the authors have steered the conversation on a logical framework that culminates in translation of concern and information into transformative action.

This approach is rooted in biblical realism, a commitment to embrace, difficult realities as part of the brokenness of God's creation and a principled refusal to waste the potential for learning and growth that our circumstances provide. In so doing, they help us transcend the common trap of the 'paralysis of analysis,' which often results in entrenchment of gloom and helplessness in discussion of matters of this nature and magnitude. As various contributors show, such a view will help people plan and strategize, shift from fixed to growth mind-sets, and take advantage of all available tools of technology while maintaining openness to the sovereign will of God and the possibilities of a better future. Such understanding will challenge the church and corporate organizations to get out of the confines of their four walls, honestly appraise their mission to society, and realign their strategy and programs in order to remain relevant in light of COVID-19 realities. By isolating three broad aspirations for social-justice interventions, the book makes bold proposals for action on priority areas of health care systems, education and fragile livelihoods. Justifiably, these may be considered the first order of business for policy makers, the development sector and other multisectoral actors and stakeholders. Importantly, the church should rediscover its call to integral mission and take its place at the vanguard of this concerted effort, by shining the candle of hope and the dream of post-COVID 19 possibilities.

With this in mind, I heartily commend this book to you. It is my prayer and hope that you not only agree with the vision of the authors, but importantly that you will take the challenge to make the adjustments necessary to seize the opportunities availed to thrive in your life and vocational context, fully persuaded that the Sovereign God is in control of COVID-19, and the future itself.

Prof. Kivutha Kibwana, Governor, Makueni County

ENDORSEMENTS

The Severe Acute Respiratory Syndrome (SARS - COVID19) has changed the world. It is yet the one greatest concern for the entire world in the 21st century. As everyone the world over debates about the nature and impact of the deadly virus, who would have dreamt of writing a book about it. This is exactly what a team of fourteen highly gifted persons sat and did. Thus, Building Hope and Resilience in the wake of a Pandemic is a realization of a great dream, the making of a chronicle of the COVDI 19 menace. This collection of well thought out and clearly researched articles regarding the Corona Virus. The diversity of the authors from a wide range of professions speaks volumes about the seriousness of this collection and the determination of the editors to ensure that most of the affected will have a lesson or two to pick from the articles. The book does not generalize issues. It addresses concerns affecting people down from the personal, familial, community to national and international levels.

Prof Wangari Mwai, Associate DVC

United States International University (USIU)

It is my pleasure to endorse such a beautiful piece of work! The writers of this book avail a collection of important reflections from various perspectives to provide appreciation of the situation caused by the global pandemic of Covid-19, to guide our adjustment to what would be the 'new normal' and to help us anticipate a hopeful post-Covid situation. We have wonderful reflections founded on godly principles challenging us to focus on what truly matters: family more than our jobs, vocation more than careers and to appreciate technology as a tool and not a master.

Dr. Esther Nyagah

Educational Leadership & Administration Expert

and Registrar Academics (Africa International University)

INTRODUCTION

On the 11th of March 2020 the WHO Director Dr. Tedros Adhanom announced that COVID-19 was no longer a disease in a small Wuhan location but a global pandemic. The news was received with foreboding concerns and questions of its spread and its effect on society and economies of nations. We got into new habits, and unprecedented uncertainty. Places of prayer were closed, cities were locked down and schools shut.

This situation found leaders and followers, teachers and learners and employers and employees walking on ground they had never been before. No one had experienced or trained on how to parent during a pandemic or how to shop or how to work from home or how to lead a team through a pandemic. It turned to be a time to think on the feet, to listen more, and to look up to the skies as the Italian Prime Minister once said expressing his desperation on the situation. In a time like this, everyone is focused on self-preservation and survival.

Yet in this situation as humans, we are building new norms that build our resilience and shape our views on what life really is. We set out to put together this book to address key questions: What are people doing to cope? What reflections are helpful in building hope at this time? What can we learn from other pandemics and crises in history that can help us walk this path now? How are families coping with new dynamics of homeschooling; how are spiritual leaders keeping their members fed spiritually? What reflections from theories on resilience are helpful now? How do we pray in the darkness of the tunnel? How do we make sense of this situation? How do we act, adapt and transform this situation for the better?

This book is a collection of articles and reflections from key leaders and experts who ardently explore the three core elements of resilience: Accept, Adapt and Act. These three elements form the 3 themes that organize the book.

On the Accept theme we have articles focusing on: Embracing change and psychosocial support; Living with purpose during uncertainties; rediscovering the human frailty and the call to repositioning our hope in God.

Adapt section takes the middle part of the book and explores: Embracing wholehearted living in order to adapt; Building resilience in children; Building courage, care and comradeship as men during the pandemic; Restoring family to order – among others.

The last part of the book focuses on Act – Acting with hope. In this section the articles delve on leadership during turbulence and how to manage change; How to build resilience for mental health during the crisis; lessons from church history in reference to pandemics; and a broad view on Post-COVID aspirations for social-economic justice. The book ends with an insightful reflection on reaffirming our hope in God and embracing the opportunities for human flourishing now and beyond the pandemic.

Growing up as a young boy in the village, we had no commercially manufactured games like our counterparts in towns and cities perhaps enjoyed. Not only that, but our parents cared little how we kept ourselves busy outside of school. Thus, we invented our own ways of keeping ourselves entertained. One way was to play games in the dust. Some of these were relatively complex, requiring setting them out on the ground for some time before the game starts. And what joy and satisfaction we felt after completing the painstaking work of setting out the ground and then embarking on the game itself. It was always worth the hard effort and we played for hours.

But I recall on several of such occasions, while at the height of enjoying our game, a whirlwind would come out of nowhere with great ferocity. It would raise up a great amount of dust and by the time it passed by in just but a few seconds, we would be left with dust in our eyes, clothes, and hair. But the worst was that it wiped out all the markings of our game and the record of our scores. The whirlwind completely disrupted our game, our joy, and in a sense our lives. Though now as an adult I do not see what the fuss was all about, at the time we were a greatly devastated and disappointed lot. Often, we abandoned the game and went our separate ways. On other occasions, we mustered our energies and redrew the game all over again.

If there is one word that may describe what Coronavirus has done to humanity across the globe, it is: Disruption. For almost every individual -- irrespective of age, gender, colour, race, or social status--the virus has disrupted our life routines, families, jobs, businesses, plans, and programs. Sadly, for some, their very lives have been snuffed off prematurely. Whereas the degree may vary from person to person, our games have been wiped off by this Corona whirlwind, thereby leaving many in a state of confusion. Many questions arise in our minds --What next? How do I navigate this situation? Will life be the same again? Where do I start?

This book is packed with insightful reflections on these critical questions. Written from a very practical perspective, herein is a timely collection of articles by respected men and women of God that will help any weary pilgrim to regain courage and strength to redraw their game of life. For example, I found the illustration by George Ogalo from the behaviour of Safari ants, after experiencing the shock of disruption of their journey, very insightful. The ability of the ants to regroup and design new paths for their onward journey, is a lesson worthy of emulation. Many such deep insights and hilarious testimonies awaits any who makes the wise choice to read this book. It is certainly a worthy read.

May I salute these saints of God for taking time in the midst of a devastating pandemic to compile this piece. You have certainly set us an example on how to deal with disruption. May it encourage us all too arise and redraw our games – Accept, Adapt, Act – for life must continue.

David Oginde (Rev) PhD, **Presiding Bishop**
Christ is the Answer Ministries (CITAM)

LIST OF CONTRIBUTORS

Roseline Olumbe, PhD Holistic Child Development Expert. Lecturer in Daystar University, School of Human and Social Sciences

Wairimu Kinuthia, Finance and Project Management Professional.

George Ogalo, A Biblical theologian. National Director at FOCUS-KENYA and Board Director an National Campaign Against Drugs and Alcohol Abuse (NACADA)

Simon Mbevi, A lawyer by training and Executive Director and Founder of Transform Nations.

Christi Byerly, A Professional Certified Coach. Christi is the CEO and director of training with Awaken Coaching Institute

Rev. Lucas Owako, A Biblical Theologian and currently works as Administrator at Africa Enterprise

Canon Francis Omondi, Priest of the Anglican Church of Kenya, of All Saints Cathedral Diocese

Rabecca Wanjiku, Information Systems Specialist and Graduate Student at the University of Cape Town (UCT)

Charity Waithima, PhD. Clinical Psychologist and Ass. Professor at United States International University (USIU)

Rev. Paul Njoroge, Senior Pastor at CITAM Clay City and Head of Social Action and Advocacy (SAAG) at CITAM

David Ewagata, Director of YHub NetworX

Pete Ondeng, Founder of Lead Africa Foundation and the Author, Africa's Moment

Mary Thamari, PhD Social Anthropologist and Development Practitioner

Joshua Wathanga, PhD A Consultant in Policy, Strategy and Corporate Governance. Board Chairman of Hesabika Trust

Julia Kagunda, PhD Counseling Psychologist and Communications Specialist and Consultant with Elim Palm Renewal Centre (EPRC)

Angela Obwaka, A Human Resource Specialist and a Faith vlogger

PART 1: ACCEPT

Stripped of our Illusions, What a Mercy

By Wairimu Kinuthia

To humans belong the plans of the heart, but from the Lord comes the proper answer of the tongue. Proverbs 16:1

The importance of planning cannot be gainsaid. There is a well-accepted maxim that 'to fail to plan is to plan to fail'. And so we plan. We plan for our organizations, for our families and our personal goals.

The thing is, we are used to having our plans work out. We buy a plane ticket for a flight weeks into the future, and on the scheduled date we are more likely to travel than not to. When we are invited for future events, we pull out our diaries and slot in the meetings and you can bet that they will happen at the appointed time. Should something unexpected come up, the meeting will be rescheduled to a definite time in future. This has led us to take our planning for granted and from experience, we know that if we establish good plans they will most probably come to pass.

At the beginning of the year I was on a flight, which had been planned, well in advance, travelling with my family from my home country to my country of residence after a holiday break. The flight had taken off on time and proved to be my kind of flight. Uneventful! Uneventful up to the point where after significant descent and almost landing, the pilot in an abrupt change of direction pointed the nose of the plane upward taking us back up into the skies. This disruption of the plan led to puzzlement on the side of the passengers and when the explanation finally came from the pilot, it did little to assuage our fears. He announced that they had encountered a problem and could not land the plane until it was resolved. In what seemed like an eternity before the plane landed, I had time enough to think about what would happen should the plane not land safely and should these be the final hours of my life. What hit me as most ironical was the sheer number of plans I had laid out for the year. I had a number of projects I was raring to execute, the list of people I planned to meet, new ideas I hoped to sell and to top it up my plan to learn a new language. It occurred to me in those tense moments that those big and well laid out plans might just come to nothing! As is said, the best-laid plans of mice and men often go awry.

That small personal experience is nothing compared to what COVID-19 has visited on the whole world. My friends spent the better part of the last six months planning their dream wedding only to be told they cannot have more than 15 people attending, a disappointment and a massive change of plans. For some people, trips that were meant to be for a short time left them stranded in foreign countries, some separated from their families for the foreseeable future.

Organisations had planned events, months, even years in advance such as product launches, conferences and other campaigns. They now find that these need to be put on the back burner as they deal with new realities.

These new realities including staff working from home or not working at all, grossly reduced or altogether cut off income and closed schools are just some of the drastic measures that changed plans. Everything suddenly is subject to how the corona virus situation evolves. We are reduced to being unable to make plans as small as when two friends can meet, when to travel or hold an event.

The current situation feels like an out of body experience where we sincerely don't know what the future holds. Off course this has always been the case, we don't know what the future holds! We had somehow convinced ourselves that by planning the future, then we know it, and that we were in control. And now when the outbreak of corona virus has paralysed the world and our individual lives, we are left with our plans in tatters and hopefully awakened to the realization that we are not in control of the future. And yet the reality is that nothing has changed. We have never really been in control of the future; we simply had the illusion that we were.

These illusions have now been exposed. We like to think that we are in charge. We make plans and execute them. Suddenly overnight, this ability is taken away. Who would have thought that it would take a virus to stop our movements and our plans? We want this to be over as quickly as possible so that we can go back to our mostly predictable lives where we have control. Those of us who are fortunate only have to wrestle with boredom and listlessness at being coped up in the house. Others feel 'zoomed out' from numerous meetings and 'scrolled up' from keeping up with COVID-19 news, enough already, our minds scream! Still yet, others wrestle with more critical matters such as drastically reduced or lost income. Uncertainty is killing us possibly because we have always convinced ourselves that we can be certain.

With regard to planning for the future, it's hard to find a more apt description or a more piercing admonition than the words of James 4: 13 -14, Now listen, you who say, "Today or tomorrow we will go to this or that city, spend a year there, carry on business and make money." Why, you do not even know what will happen tomorrow. What is your life? You are a mist that appears for a little while and then vanishes. Instead, you ought to say, "If it is the Lord's will, we will live and do this or that."

James wrote those words in a letter to a church that was experiencing hardships. Scattered due to persecution, he aimed to encourage them to remain faithful and show the radical life implications of faith. In a tone that sounds almost sarcastic he says, "wait a minute, what is it with your big plans, how preposterous!" The Christians were making plans, which of course is, the wise thing to do. The Bible itself affirms the wisdom of planning and thinking ahead. Proverbs 20:18 says "Plans succeed through good counsel while Proverbs 21:5 says, "Good planning and hard work lead to prosperity, but hasty shortcuts lead to poverty". The problem that is being addressed, therefore, cannot be planning. The problem seems to be that even though they had professed faith, there were parts of their lives where they lived as if God didn't exist.

Since the bible is not against planning, the problem is when we work, plan and prepare without considering God, which is the sin of presumption. This means that we have forgotten God. Forgetting God can only mean one thing: that we have put ourselves in the place of God. This ultimately means that we believe we know what's best and what the future holds. James bluntly points out just how ridiculous this thinking is! "...yet you do not know what tomorrow will bring." And when we assume that we do, even for a moment, it is, as James would say, the height of arrogance! This is a big contrast to God's words in Isaiah 55:8-9, "For my thoughts are not your thoughts, neither are your ways my ways", declares the Lord. For as the heavens are higher than the earth, so are my ways higher than your ways and my thoughts than your thoughts."

When we plan without considering God, we assume that we 'know' what the future holds, and also that we are actually in 'control' of our future! In living this way, as if we 'know the future' we assume God's omniscience, and when we live as if we 'control' the future we assume that we are all-powerful. James helps us get perspective here of our lives in perspective of eternity: "What is your life? You are a mist that appears for a little time then vanishes." In the context of all eternity, our lives are like a blip on the screen. This doesn't mean our lives don't have meaning or that they don't count for anything, but it means that we derive our meaning from the eternal God and not on our own!

So, when we have been busy updating our planners and calendars something happened that we did not plan for! Corona virus happened, a pandemic that has in an unbelievably short time, gripped the whole world. This has happened at the start of a new year while our resolutions are still fresh and we are still energized and optimistic about meeting our annual targets. It has made a mockery of our big plans for tomorrow and made short work of our presumption that our tomorrows are under control. This has revealed a fallacy that we hide so well that we could deny it exists; the fallacy is that we know what will happen tomorrow. The truth is that we don't know the future. Our response when plans change depends on what we believe about how much we control. The responses will vary from apathetic resignation with a shoulder-shrugging Inshallah to rage and blaming those whose ineptness we believe has caused the change in plans. This kind of anger has been evident especially in social media with blaming being generously heaped on those who we believe could have protected us from this virus. We blame the government and the police, and we listen to theories implicating many others for the situation we find ourselves in.

Other by-products of this fallacy include worry or anxiety when things don't go as we think they should. Timothy Keller (Sermon "Worry" 1996) says, "Worry is a frustrated aspiration to omniscience. Worry is saying "I know and I'm concerned God won't get it right". When things do go as planned it produces pride (I "knew" and I "controlled"). This pride in our lives can result in a false sense of security that eventually when it is all said and done, will only lead us to despair. Our pride can lead to despair when things stop going our way and we realize that the control we thought we had was just an illusion.

It's then a high time to address the question that James poses, "What then is your life?" Maybe we think that the number of successful plans that we execute can be used to measure life's value. Jesus talked about the rich man who made his great plans for the future, and foolishly lost it all when his soul was required of him (Luke 12:16-21). James does not mince his words as he described how brief, frail and transient life is. "…a mist that appears for a little while and then vanishes". On the COVID-19 tracker platforms, we have watched in shocked disbelief as the numbers of those infected and those who have died continue to soar day after day. Nothing could have brought us more face to face with our mortality than the pictures and video clips being shared of rows upon rows of coffins lined up and waiting for interment. In Shakespeare's words, "Out, out, brief candle! Life's but a walking shadow, a poor player that struts and frets his hour upon the stage and is heard no more". And in the Psalmist's words, "Yet you sweep people away in the sleep of death they are like the new grass of the morning: In the morning it springs up new, but by evening it is dry and withered". (Psalms 90:5-6)

After painting that picture of the futility of life, James gives a way out, "Instead, you ought to say, "If it is the Lord's will (Deo Volente), we will live and do this or that." Not simply as a phrase to tag at the end of our conversations, but to remember that we are dependent on God for all things. If the problem is that we've 'forgotten' God, then the solution is to 'remember' Him. Our heart's posture should be one that has God at the forefront of all that we do. We remember that He is the King of Kings and Lord of Lords; that He is sovereignly working in our lives and in the words of Abraham Kuyper (1880) "that there is not one square inch in all of creation in which He doesn't declare, "It is mine". We remember that if he can be trusted with our eternal salvation, then He can be trusted with our jobs, children, finances, and whatever else causes us to fear and be anxious.

My flight mishap at the beginning of the year brought me face to face with how easily plans can fail midflight. I, fortunately, got home safely and had the opportunity to reflect on the words from James about planning for the future. I recognized the fact that my life is but a mist and I have no guarantee for the future, even with all the good reasons for me to always plan. I, therefore, choose to continue planning to the best of my ability and with all the tools at my disposal. Yet I choose to cultivate deep thankfulness to God for each and every day that I lived and every plan that came to fruition. I also choose to more than ever, prayerfully entrust each and every plan to God and to trust Him, especially when the plans seem to fail. It is in particularly the plans that fail that I have been challenged to trust God's goodness and sovereignty and His promise that in all things God works for the good of those who love him, who have been called according to his purpose (Romans 8:28).

As we sit with our plans in shambles and without any illusions of certainty as to when or whether we shall be able to resume our plans, I dare say that this could be tender mercy from God. A reminder that we don't wield the control that we think we do over our lives. It could be a time to repent and be delivered from the sin of presumption. It is a call to make all our plans with a constant awareness of the hand of God and a proper estimation of our limitations. Apostle Paul knew and lived this principle as we read in Acts 18:21 "I will return again to you, God willing", 1 Corinthians 4:19 "But I will come to you shortly, if the Lord wills" and 1 Corinthians 16:7 "I hope to stay a while with you, if the Lord permits".

May this revelation of how out of control we are lead us back to the one who is really in control and has always been. As we remain housebound and unable to implement a lot of what filled our diaries, may we accept in humility that God is in control and that God knows the future and that we can trust him completely! When we are tempted to fret, worry and doubt, let these serve as pointers to the idols of our lives. The things we hold most important and believe we must have for life to have any meaning such as certainty and control. May we receive this unexpected mercy from God during these uncertain times and be rid of these idols. In the interim season, Corona virus has not only taken our ability to predictably plan and execute our plans, it has threatened to take away our very lives. May we put our hope in a sovereign God, one who is in charge of every bit of history.

May we rest in the true security that comes from our sovereign and resurrected Savior Jesus Christ!

What mercy?
What mercy is this
What rending of kindness?
That we in weakness
Find mercy as this?
How we clench our plans
Pitching for the nest lane
How we invest in futility
Forgetting our frailty
What mercy is this
What rending of love
That we in our frailty
We find mercy as this
Where now can we hide?
Where on earth is refuge?
Which space are we to cower?
Which hope is there to clutch?
What mercy is this?
What rending of grace?
That our face is turned to His
That our hope is stayed on Him

Living Purposefully in the Light of Finitude

Dr Joshua Wathanga

In responding to the question of "What is God doing through the Coronavirus?", John Piper (2020) proposes six possible answers and one of them is that "the coronavirus is God's thunderclap call for all of us to repent and realign our lives with the infinite worth of Christ". Piper contends that "the global scope and seriousness of the coronavirus is too great for God to waste". In effect, God is giving us all - individually, our families, church, nation, and the nations- an opportunity to hear him afresh, to repent, learn, and recalibrate our lives in the light of our mortality – our finitude.

If you believe, as I do, that our heavenly Father is loving, not malicious, then it follows that every experience he allows us to go through is for our good. As Romans 8:28 teaches us, "we know that God works all things together for the good of those who love Him, who are called according to His purpose" (Berean Study Bible). If a loving heavenly Father allows us to go through a tragic experience in order for us to learn, and we don't learn, your guess is as good as mine as to what he should do: He will give you another chance to learn by offering you a resit or repeat experience! That is why I take my bad or difficult experiences so seriously that I note in my daily journaling the circumstances, how God has delivered me, and what I have learned from them. I must say that the fear of a repeat helps me sense the likelihood of failing again from a mile away, but keeping notes on how God has delivered me before helps me to appropriate His help sooner.

A pandemic like coronavirus is too great for God to waste, and neither should we. As I have reflected on what God is reminding me and wanting me to relearn, re-align, and re-calibrate in my life, there are at least six lessons that come to mind. I hope you will find some, if not all, of these lessons helpful for you as well.

You are here on earth for a purpose

Many of us go through life without clarifying what we are living for or we simply immerse ourselves into whatever life throws at us without pausing to reflect on why God placed us here. Are we here simply to be born, eat, work, reproduce, and then die? One way of maximizing the opportunity the coronavirus pandemic offers us is to reflect more deeply on why God placed us here on earth at this time.

In his classic book, The Purpose Driven Life, Rick Warren (1997) notes that "the purpose of your life is far greater than your own personal fulfilment, your peace of mind, or even your happiness. It's far greater than your family, your career, or even your wildest dreams and ambitions. If you want to know why you were placed on this planet, you must begin with God. You were born by his purpose and for his purpose."

It is easy to confuse the jobs we do with purpose. Dr Nicholas Pearce (2019) differentiates between career (the job we do) with vocation (the purpose for which we live). Purpose is not what we do, but why it matters. Pearce advises that in order to find out your "why", ask yourself: "what is it that brings me deep joy and fulfilment? What problems do I want to solve? What is it that I would do if

I never got paid another day?" Vocation is far more about a greater Why than it is about a particular What, because the What will shift with time.

According to Frederick Buechner (2017), "vocation is the place where your deep gladness and world's deep hunger meet". Similarly, Parker Palmer (2000) writes, "Today I understand vocation quite differently - not as a goal to be achieved but as a gift to be received. Discovering vocation does not mean scrambling toward some prize just beyond my reach but accepting the treasure of true self I already possess. Vocation does not come from a voice "out there" calling me to become something I am not. It comes from a voice "in here" calling me to be the person I was born to be, to fulfil the original selfhood given me at birth by God."

Live with the end in mind

If I then understand that I am not a cosmic accident and that I am placed here by a divine being with a purpose for my life, that changes everything! It follows that I will live my life with the end in mind. In coaching, as we also do in strategic planning, we focus on the end-game and ask questions like: "What is your vision of success? What impact do you want to have in 15 years? What is your Vision 2030?" Once it is clearer what goal or outcomes you are working towards, we then work backwards and ask questions of what it will take to achieve those results and what milestones will mark success. In effect, we should not plan forwards (I will do this or study this subject so that I become or I achieve such and such), but rather backwards (because this is the impact or outcomes I want to see, or this is the difference I am called to make, I will study or do such and such in order to get there!). When I discovered this way of thinking and planning, it changed my entire perspective on my life and work planning. Bob Buford (2008) calls living with the end in mind "writing your epitaph" and "articulating a strategy of multiplying your contribution".

Living with the end in mind must not be confused with the Machiavellian philosophy that the ends justify the means. On the contrary, vocation, or living on purpose, is not about a destination – what we want to become- but a process- of becoming. As Dr Pearce[1] observes, vocation is about who you are becoming as much as it is about what you are doing. Our lives should be much more a quest and much less an endpoint. The quest is making our best better than it was before.

Set goals for your life, not just your job

If we now understand that your purpose in life is greater than your job, you can see that it is even more important to set goals for your vocation than your career. Many of us only practice the planning in the workplace and just go through life from day to day without much thought or plan. Since I first read Rick Warren's Purpose-Driven Life, my perspective on life-planning completely changed. He notes that most people struggle with three basic issues in life: Who am I? – a question of identity; Do I matter? – a question of importance; What is my place in life? – a question of impact. Warren[2] notes that the answers to these questions are found in God's five purposes for our lives and these are as follows: First, "What will be the centre of my life?" Warren notes that this is the question of worship. Who are you going to live for? What will I build my life around? Career, family, money, having fun? None of these things are strong enough to hold your life together. Whatever is in the centre of your life is your god

[1] Pearce, 136
[2] Warren, 201

(or God if it is Christ). The second question Warren notes is, "What will be the character of my life?" This is the question of discipleship. What kind of person will you be? God is far more interested in what you are rather than what you do. You will take your character into eternity, but not your career. Make a list of the character qualities you want to develop and start working on them.

The third question Warren notes is, "What will be the contribution of my life?" This is a question of service. What will be your ministry in the body of Christ? Knowing what is in your S.H.A.P.E (Spiritual Gifts, Heart, Abilities, Personality, and Experiences) will help you know the best role for you. Even Jesus did not meet the needs of everyone. What can you do best? The fourth question is, "What will be the communication of my life? This is a question of mission to unbelievers. What five or so life lessons or godly passions can you share with others? God may give you a special target group of people to focus your reaching out – say children, or our age mates, or college students. And the fifth question Warren suggests is, "What will be the community of my life?" This is a question of fellowship. How will I demonstrate my commitment to other believers and connection to the family of God? The more you mature, the more you will love the body of Christ and want to sacrifice for, and give resources for the work of God. These various questions suggest that you need to set goals for your life so that you can grow in each of these five purposes. I have personally found it very useful to constantly reflect on these questions and streamline my plans and actions accordingly.

Grow in your emotional intelligence
I had not understood the importance of emotional intelligence (EQ), and what it was until I came across

"Emotional Intelligence" written by Daniel Goleman (1996). The question Goleman posed and set to answer was, "Why is it that a small percentage of leaders develop to their fullest potential while most leaders hit a plateau far beneath what one might expect of them?" According Goleman, the difference has to do with self-leadership or emotional intelligence. This form of self-leadership is exhibited by leaders when they refuse to give up during times of crisis, when they manage to hold ego at bay, when they stay focused on their mission rather than being distracted by other people's agenda. These exceptional leaders know their strengths, their limits, and their weaknesses. Research by Goleman (2004) shows that the exceptional performance of leaders can be explained more by EQ than IQ. That may explain why most senior jobs attach a higher premium to person specifications or competency frameworks than skills and knowledge. IQ may get you a job, but the success will be determined by your EQ.

When researching on living on purpose and emotional intelligence, I came across a TedTalk video entitled, "How to Know your Life Purpose in 5 minutes" by Adam Leipzig (2013), former Disney Executive and CEO of Entertainment Media Partners. Talking of his 25th Yale University Reunion, he says of his astounding discovery of his former college mates that 80% of them were unhappy with their lives: "I feel as if have wasted life and I am half way through it; I don't know what my life is about." Now these were not people without good education and jobs: they were Yale graduates, one of the most prestigious universities in the world! These were people in positions of power, wealth, and prestige. The 20% who were happy had some interesting things in common: They knew who they were (identity); what they did - what they loved to do and were supremely qualified and passionate about; and who they it did for and what these people wanted or they needed, and finally, how these people changed as a result of what you gave them.

The Yale example illustrates the outworking of Emotional intelligence through life. EQ has four domains: self-awareness; self-management; social awareness and social skills. The good news is that one can learn and grow in emotional intelligence if we are going to be better leaders of ourselves, and of others.

Be a life-long disciple and learner

Champions don't become champions in the ring, they are recognized there. If you want to see where someone develops into a champion, look at his or her daily routine. In his audio book, "Leadership 101", John Maxwell (2003) gives the example of Theodore Roosevelt who became one of the most admired and effective US Presidents. He was one of the toughest mentally and physically although he didn't start that way. As a child he was very sickly with asthma and poor eyesight and his parents were not sure he would survive. When he was 12, he started spending time everyday building his body and mind. He worked out with weights, ice-skating and boxing. He went to study at Harvard, later became City Police Commissioner for New York and later President of the United States. His accomplishments were remarkable and under his leadership, the US became a superpower. He kept learning and growing and improving himself and in time became a strong leader.

If you look at your last week's schedule, how much of it did you devote to regular, disciplined activities? Did you do anything to improve yourself spiritually, professionally? Did you engage in activities promoting good health?

Did you make good use of your income or improve your investments? Or do you keep putting these things off? As Jackson Brown is quoted to have said, "Talent without discipline is like an octopus on roller skates. There is plenty of movement, but you never know if it's going to be forward, backwards, sideways".

As one committed to life-long learning, surround yourself with mentors and people smarter than you. Seek to be continually inspired by something, learning what your triggers are. Henry Ford once said: "I am not the smartest, but I surround myself with competent people." According to leadership literature, successful leaders surround themselves with good people, but great leaders surround themselves with people who are even better than they are.

Run your race with integrity

When your values and actions are aligned, then you are running your race with integrity: "Integrity is about oneness, wholeness; it means that your actions are consistent with your values. It means that the values you say you have guide your decisions.[3]" For many of us, there is a mismatch between what we say is valuable and the reality of how we spend our time, resources and opportunities. Then the goals we are pursuing violate our values. Followers will only trust leaders who exhibit highest levels of integrity. Every time you compromise character, you compromise leadership. Even small things matter like keeping or not keeping your word, keeping time; this kind of things can demoralize your team.

In the book of Genesis, we see that Joseph remained uncorrupted by power. He avoided financial impropriety, political scandals, and sexual seduction. He stayed

---

[3] Pearce, 111.

unstained to the end. Joseph must have lived with the daily awareness that leaders must possess high degree of moral authority if they are going to lead well. People will follow your leadership if they have confidence they are not going to wind up in a ditch and you are not going to lead a double life, or steal the company's cash or the church offering! People need confidence in your integrity.

We started by quoting John Piper that "a pandemic like coronavirus is too great for God to waste" and that God is giving us all – individually, our families, church, nation, and the nations- an opportunity to hear him afresh, to repent, learn, and recalibrate our lives in the light of our mortality – our finitude. In this chapter, I have suggested six lessons that we can learn so that we can live purposeful and God-honoring lives – clarifying and living your purpose, clarify your outcomes, set the goals, grow in your emotional intelligence, keep s long-life discipleship and learning posture, and run the race with integrity.

BIBLIOGRAPHY

Brown, J. (n.d.). From https://www.brainyquote.com/quotes/h_jackson_brown_jr_134502

Buechner, F. (2017, July 18). From https://www.frederickbuechner.com/quote-of-the-day/2017/7/18/vocation

Buford, B. (2008). Halftime: Moving from Success to Significance. Grand Rapids, Michigan: Zondervan.

Ford, H. (n.d.). From http://www.ft.lk/columns/surround-yourself-with-the-best-people-you-can-find/4-69735

Goleman, D. (1996). Emotional Intelligence: Why it Can Matter More Than IQ. Bloomsbury.

Goleman, D. (2004, January). What Makes a Leader? Harvard Business Review , 1-10.

Leipzig, A. (2013, February 1). How to Know Your Life Purpose in 5 Minutes. From https://youtu.be/vVsXO9brK7M?list=PL5qZYippVH6nQWgF4jhUOZEAPRsx0df_A

Maxwell, J. C. (2003, January 3). Leadership 101.

Palmer, P. J. (2000). Let Your Life Speak: Listening for the Voice of Vocation. John Wiley & Sons, Inc.

Pearce, N. (2019). The Purpose Path: A Guide to Pursuing Your Authentic Work. New York: St Martin's Press.

Piper, J. (2020). Coronavirus and Christ. Wheaton, IL: Crossway.

Warren, R. (1997). What am I Here For? The Purpose Driven Life. Zondervan.

Change is here: Expect and Embrace it

By Pastor David Ewagata, Director of YHub NetworX

Psalm 11:3 asks a very fundamental question:

"When the foundations are being destroyed, what can the righteous do?" (NIV). "What can an honest person do when everything crumbles?" (CEV)

Years ago, during the days of the "Cold war", the American army came up with an acronym defining the state of things in the world of war, espionage and counter-espionage at that time. The term was, "VUCA", standing for, Volatility, Uncertainty, Complexity, and Ambiguity. If there is a time in the recent history of humanity that this acronym best describes, it is now. In a space of three months, world business, learning, travel, work, governance, faith, and many other 'norms', have been adversely affected by one single invisible enemy. Oil prices have plummeted and continue to plummet to levels unseen before. At the writing of this, the oil prices in the US have gone on a negative. Nobody knows what exactly the source of this virus is and speculations, theories, narratives and counter-narratives are rife. Worse still, no one knows the end of it all. Is this the decimation of the world or just a hiccup in the grand scheme of things? Is this the onset of the last days, the introduction of the new world order, the curtain raiser of a neo-colonial control system? Who knows?

What then must we do?

Rampant attempts to 'do something' are as human as it gets. When I was in high school, we had a near catastrophe. On one night, we were in our classrooms for extended studies in the evning. It was raining softly and there seemed to be nothing to betray a usual evening. Then, out of the blues, the entire campus lit up and followed up, almost simultaneously by the deafening sound of thunder as lightning struck! For a split second, everything inside and outside the classroom was so bright, followed by pitch darkness, and then came the roar of thunder. It had never been as clear and close as I experienced it that day. What followed was pandemonium as people scampered for safety through the one little door in each classroom. Desks and chairs were falling all over as people fled the scene.

What followed was dramatic: screaming, panic-running, falling, tripping, tears, confusion, and all manner of high adrenalin moves. Then slowly, reality, sense, calm, understanding, and order returned. People began to check on the same people they ran over a few moments ago. Some had injuries some were shaken, and some were coming to terms with each other's reactions and now just laughing their fears out as we realized that the danger moment was over.

Was it a really dangerous thing? Yes, it was. Was it a real direct threat? Yes! In fact, a tree that was hit literally dried up to the root and had to be cut down the very next morning lest it falls on a building! Incidentally, everyone who got injured- was as a result of the stampede, and certainly not directly the lightning. It is the people tripping over each other that caused injuries. It is the desks and chairs that became weapons in our moments of reaction. It was the scramble at the door made pulp of others..

We all acknowledge that when a crisis happens, we tend to lose all sense of it. Sometimes we can't locate the emergency door, or stay calm. Frantic defines the new calm.

Several mantras have been coined to heap even more pressure on an already bad situation that has tipped the entire globe off balance. The big question on everyone's mind is, "What should I do to survive, cope, adapt, adjust, thrive, or incarnate?" '

Another big challenge behind the big question is the proverbial lack of a distinct definition of 'IT'. What is 'IT'? Who defines whether you got 'IT'? What is the true measure of 'IT'?

Change is here

"Forget the former things; do not dwell in the past. See, I am doing a new thing! Now it springs up; do you not perceive it? I am making a way in the desert, and streams in the wasteland" (Isaiah 43:18-19). If there is a time that this scripture takes on life-size presence, it is now. Our anticipation of the future realities may well play into the following 4 categories:

1. **It will be the same again. Resist change**

The great thing about this view is the sense of hope that it holds. The posture is that 'this too shall pass'. In the meantime, people put temporary measures and hope normalcy returns as soon as possible. Even if things normalize, for sure the events of these past few months have greatly altered a vast portion of our lives.

These people resent change. They had plans made for the next two years and just can't imagine having to go back to the drawing boards.

Many melancholies fall into this space. Long-term planning is their forte and so interruption of process is a dreadful thing. The need to know and have control overwhelms you and you cannot imagine not being aware of the next step. I spoke to one such character and she was besides herself because her plans for next year were being thrown off. I tell her, the whole human system is off the chain so it is not as bad as if she were the only one lying in a bed somewhere as the world goes on. But no, I needed to be here, done this, gone there, by that time. Hard as it may be, what you need to do is take a breath. The whole earth is breathing too.

2. **It may never be the same again. Suspect change**

I love the innocence of this category. Unfortunately, this stance does not allow us to venture into a transformative mode but rather resign to fate. The mantra for this category is best captured by the lyrics of an old time classic by Doris Day, "Que sera, sera, whatever will be, will be, the future is not ours to see…"

The phlegmatic finds a place in this category more than any other temperament. There is a sense of anticipation coupled with a little preparation- just in case. Their joy is that finally people can see the sense in just sitting back and watching things unfold without our frantic impactions. Suspicion is not a strategy and so these may have to lean in a bit more and grasp what needs to be done.

3. **It should never be the same again. Expect change**

We are very good at this when it comes to pointing fingers at others. At this time, we have the opportunity to take a very introspective journey. If in our closets we cannot realize the folly of our ways and the frothiness of life, we have failed to do what all of us in our basics should be able to attain- a choice to do right.

The pandemic has given us reflective space- something our cities, our education, our work, our relationships or the lack thereof, have totally robbed us of for many years. If we haven't tasted something sweet in the reprieve, then we most likely we go back and repeat the same mistakes, run at the same pace, and do the same things that this opportunity has granted us to change.

Sanguines love this season. Its new, its unpredictable, it offers a fresh challenge, and all their undone work is now covered in the shuffle of the disruption! Their stress point in all this is the fact that they cannot connect with people as intimately as they would like to but have made vast compensations through social media platforms. Any attention is good attention. Their biggest challenge is the unpreparedness for what comes and sometimes, after an excitement-filled day, they retire to bed afraid because they spent it all and have no contingency plan if things press on as they are.

4. **It will never be the same again. Embrace change.**

This is my prayer. If we can step into the seven mountains of influence or what we call the seven spheres of society with this mindset, we can rebuild our homes, our schools, our hospitals, our nation, our entertainment, our businesses, why, even our churches- yes, our churches- on the right foundation! Simply put, "Things must never be the same again!"

This is the cup of tea of the Choleric. They may not know what the new season will look like but they are sure of one thing, they will be in charge when it's all over. This sense of resolve that takes advantage of the crisis to step forward and lead is absolutely necessary especially in spaces where things have not been running well- which is largely everywhere.

Conclusion

When the reset button is hit, it's meant to restore a system with the best possible chance for a proper set-up. It will be a major waste for us to go through a Covid-19 season only to go back to our old ways! May we, with all honesty, take advantage of this time to reset our lives to the proper parameters.

For example, education for our children must not be about simply acquiring information, but building character; This may help us fix the pool from which poor leadership is derived.

Perhaps kitchen gardens should not be for luxury anymore, but an opportunity to produce healthy food. There should be a new pacing of life, with more regular physical exercise.

The Media and entertainment industry should not be all about the decadence, wickedness, and the celebration of shame. It should be a wholesome, restorative, convicting, driving, changing vehicle.

Hard work and service must be to our families, our communities, our needy, our nation, and ultimately, our God. This pandemic has even taught us that we cannot keep our families running on autopilot as we push our careers to the limit.

Technology is Thrilling but Humanity will Always be First

By Rabecca Wanjiku, Graduate Student in IT Systems, University of Cape Town

The year is 2020 and everything is fast and furious. We have rockets that can take more people and cargo to space. We have a bullet train that travels at 430km/h. We can fly around the globe in 46hrs. More than half of the world's population has smartphones and Internet. Cryptocurrency and digital currencies are being touted as alternatives to physical money. We are even considering recreational trips to Mars. We are unstoppable. Or so we thought.

On March 12th and 13th 2020, I attended a summit in Johannesburg dubbed 4IR Digital Skills. One of the keynote speakers, a prolific researcher and futurist, delivered a lecture about where we are in the Fourth Industrial Revolution (4IR) and where we are heading to. Some of the things he said were exciting, some were surreal. Among other things, he said the children being born now may live up to 200 years because stem cell and gene editing technologies will be able to prevent or treat a lot of diseases and conditions. Like a good young person of this generation, I was tweeting per minute during the lecture, sharing with the world these mind-blowing possibilities I was hearing about our near future—a future with less suffering.

Two days after the conference, there was a sudden twist

as all public gatherings were banned in South Africa due to COVID-19. I could no longer go to the university where I study. A week and a half later, the entire country was placed under a lockdown. Things were happening fast. While I tried to adjust to working from home with the abruptness of the orders, my mind was reeling with irony. How can the world, at this point in time, be caught unaware and held hostage by a virus? A mere virus! I probably have been more scared about a hypothetical alien invasion than I ever was about a global viral pandemic. If you had surveyed the world for which between the two was more probable, I bet very few people would have thought that a respiratory viral disease would be the one to bring the world to its knees in the 21st century. In the context of Covid-19 the good and the downside of technology has been magnified further.

Technology as a double-edge sword

Technology has changed the way we live and work. But it is a double-edged sword. In some ways, it has made life better, in other ways worse. It has made life more efficient compared to pre-industrial civilizations, but it has also made us more disconnected from each other as we get more glued to all sorts of devices and schedules facilitated smoothly by cutting edge technology. Research has shown that the gradual increase in screen-time reduces social skills necessary for one on one relationships (Steve Rose 2019). As a result, even though there is a plethora of platforms to connect with old friends and strangers with whom we share common interests, young adults are currently more predisposed to loneliness than any other age group. This quote from Jean Twenge's book iGen paints a clearer picture: "In the next decade we may see more young people who know just the right emoji for a situation—but not the right facial expression." (Twenge

2017)

We have come to depend on technology and its ability to solve all our problems. When COVID-19 arrived, it pressed pause on our show. Things we did not imagine possible such as closure of our sophisticated economic, educational and entertainment institutions happened. We have been sent home to ourselves and to our families. Whether staying home means working from home or a break from work, some reflections are inevitable for all of us.

Thinking about the ways of preventing spread of a disease, staying at home, is the most basic of things which might have even sounded ridiculous at the beginning. The rest of the measures were as simple: wash your hands; don't touch your face; practice coughing and sneezing etiquette; be mindful of older and vulnerable people; and stay at home. You would think that at a time when it is possible to talk to your fridge and see the world in 7D that there probably would be a device that would have been quickly assembled and distributed across the world that can instantly detect the virus in your house and annihilate it. Sadly, that is only a sci-fi movie tale. The best available solutions have been all about being a good human being, clean, considerate and obedient.

Technology is important and it is playing a very crucial role now. Unlike pandemics in previous centuries where isolated and quarantined people had no contact with their families, we can still have virtual face to face conversations with our loved ones. Many more people would have lost their jobs if the current online collaboration tools were not in place. Advanced technologies in the medical field will expedite the development of a vaccine to deliver it sooner than would have been possible in past decades.

And there is entertainment too. We cannot underplay the role of comic relief at such a time when life as we know it has grinded to a halt and uncertainty of where we go from here looms.

Technology is an amplifier. Now more than ever is the time to watch out what it amplifies from within us. Stuck at home, most people now have more time in their hands that they do not know what to do with. People are anxious about their investments, jobs, education, health and the future in general. Technology in various forms from television to social media, like Pennywise the clown, has a lot of exciting things to offer. There's enough news to keep you glued on a screen from morning to evening. There are enough television shows and blockbusters to make you forget what month or year we are in once you start binging. There are enough games to carry you into other realms and make you forget that there is a pandemic going on. Consumption of adult content has shot up by double digits across the world since March. Technology is doing what it does best, give, give, give.

But what does it take? A lot of studies in recent years have shown that even though we have more channels of connecting with each other, we are in actual sense less connected. So close yet so far away from each other. Time spent on gadgets has compromised learning essential hands-on life skills and good habits such as reading and physical exercise. Gadgets and TV have become solutions to quell children tantrums and keep them preoccupied. A person in distress has tonnes of escape mechanisms to distract them from facing the real issues they need to address.

How about Technology Hygiene?

Just as COVID-19 has drawn our attention to handwashing

hygiene, this is also a good opportunity to evaluate our technological hygiene. Technology, even social media, can be a force for good at a personal and societal level. Benefits of more connectivity online have also been documented. Epicurus said, "Be moderate in order to taste the joys of life in abundance." (A-Z Quotes) The difference between two people using the same platform and one comes out lonelier than the other lies in the usage. Precisely, the 'social comparison orientation' has been highlighted in research. Put simply, it is when one scrolls social media feeds compulsively and based on other people's photos and statuses feels that other people have better bodies, relationships, jobs, gadgets, et cetera. This results in loss of self-esteem, irritability, and even depression.

Other indicators of technology capture include restlessness when there's limited or no internet access; checking social media first thing in the morning; spending a disproportionate amount of time on social media compared to your primary activity such as working or studying; checking the phone after each message notification; closely monitoring your posts for likes and comments; getting frustrated if you can't get a good picture from an event, meal, or outfit to post. These, among others, are pointers of high dependency (Urban Balance 2019).

As a result of Covid-19, we hopefully have a rare opportunity to do introspection and make some amends. We don't have the daily pressures at work or school to conform. Scrolling social media or gaming when bored or lonely can be replaced with reading a book, journaling, art, exercise or making a proper meal. As with any other dependency, such adjustment would hardly come easily but the change will come in small doses, like leaving your phone at home when going for a walk. There are apps that are helping with such social media rationing goals by blocking access to a platform if the predefined daily limit is reached (Steve Altrogge 2018). The best support though in any kind of transition is the people closest, who happen to be available in the extended period of pandemic restrictions. Instead of escaping to the many alternatives technology provides, be vulnerable with family and friends instead. It is an opportunity to build relationships, mend some broken chords, forge stronger unions and support each other in creating new habits. It is an opportunity to connect with children and do things with them that they will remember their whole life. It is an opportunity for silence and meditation, to search our souls and find the things that ail us. It can also be a time to connect with God better.

Even if we put no checks to our tech habits, the highspeed internet and an unlimited supply of educational and entertainment content is seemingly not enough to keep us calm indoors. That is why people in lockdowns have resorted to creative ways of connecting with others. In Italy, people started standing outside their balconies and singing together and soon other places followed. Spanish police decided to serenade people in their homes. New York residents are hosting parties where people get out and dance from their front yards. There are all sorts of tales of adaptation of life at home, most of them equally heart-warming and rib-cracking. In some places, charity drives have been started in big and small scales dedicated to those whose sources of livelihood have been cut off. Those who have plenty are sharing with those who cannot meet basic needs. In essence, it is not sophisticated technology that is anchoring and satisfying the needs in a pandemic situation. It the moments our our connection with each other that brings completes our need.

Therefore, this is an opportunity to look at technology for what it really is: a tool, just a tool. Tools are to be used for our benefit; they should not be given power to subdue us. We can use technology in this time to invent solutions to COVID-19-related problems or others. We can use it to connect with one another and spread love and hope. We can use it to remain productive and faithful employees and students. We can use it to fundraise and send help to those who are having it harder than us. We can use it to learn a new skill or language. Because of advances in technology, we are certainly in a better position to survive than any other generation that has lived through a global pandemic.

Technology is a powerful tool, but no matter how technologically advanced we are as human race, our survival does and will always depend first on our humanity.

Oh yes, no thanks, Tech
Oh yes, possibilities galore
Opportunities in plenteous
A daze here and click there
Oh, yes Tech in bounteous
No thanks, Tech
You hold our breath away
You take us to miles away
You chime on clicks all day
But no thanks, Tech
Oh yes, Tech
With copious prospects
And numerous predictions
A panorama of dictums
Oh yes, Tech is lavish
No thanks, Tech
Give me good old humans

Hand me a solid human smile
A loud human touch
Served in warm humanness
No thanks, Tech

REFERENCES

Steve Rose 2019 The power of social connection https://steverosephd.com/is-social-media-making-us-less-social/

Urban Balance 2019 Signs of social media addiction https://urbanbalance.com/signs-social-media-addiction

Steve Altrogge 2018 Apps to help you focus and block distractions https://zapier.com/blog/stay-focused-avoid-distractions/

Twenge, Jean M. 2017. IGEN: Why Today's Super-Connected Kids Are Growing up Less Rebellious, More Tolerant, Less Happy-- and Completely Unprepared for Adulthood and (What This Means for the Rest of Us). New York: Atria Books.

Red Scarlet: Embracing Psychosocial Support

By Julia Kagunda, Communication and Psychology Specialist

On this day, she could not help but the flashes kept going back and forth. Rahab had to come to terms with the fact that she was also considered a prostitute. Nobody could believe that she had left the 'profession'. But the issue of being labelled as a prostitute was not at the top of her mind on this fateful day. Her mind was obsessed with the thoughts of her safety during that season of calamity. "Will they save me and my household?' she wondered, as the war drumbeats became more pronounced. One more time she peeped through her window to see if the red scarlet cord could be seen. Indeed, it was visible but as she was putting her head back, the story replayed again for the third time.

She recalled that it all started after a long night when two men dashed into her house, whom she rebuked sharply. However, after realizing that they had come from a foreign land, she paid keen attention to their story. As they talked, she started nodding her head; it was making sense. She recalled hearing about this tribe that had come from Egypt, whom their God had dried up the water of the Red Sea and how He had fought their battles. Strangely, they also seemed to accept her without 'expecting anything in return', which was odd, considering her trade at the time. She was a well-known prostitute.

As she continued to meditate on the events of that day, she recalled how the king of Jericho had sent two men into her house to look for the spies, and how she had quickly managed to hide the two men on top of her roof and covered them with stalks of flax. When the men who had been sent by the king asked her about the whereabouts of the spies, she calmly said, "Yes, they came. At dusk, when it was time to close the city gate, they left. I have no idea where they went; go after them and you might catch up with them." (Joshua 2:5-7) Looking confused, the two men left hurriedly. But as soon as they left, she went up to the roof, where she had hidden the two men under the stalks of flax. With a soft voice, she told them, "swear to me that you will show kindness to my family when you conquer this land." With that they reached an agreement, a treaty that bound them together. The red scarlet cord carried the weight of treaty made on that day. No wonder Rahab had to be sure that it was visible.

Jericho was about to be destroyed by the Israelites but there was a treaty between one individual and the whole nation of Israel. However, the treaty was not binding unless all the binding transactions were followed. On the part of Rahab, the two spies had told her that to be protected from the Jericho conquest, she had to tie the red scarlet cord in the window through which she had let down the two spies. Additionally, her family was to be protected on one condition- that they remained in the confines of her house. If they were willing to be in that confinement, their blood was to remain on the heads of two spies if they got hurt. At the same time there was a secret oath; if she betrayed the Israelites, they were going to be released from the oath.

On the other hand, the two spies listened to Rahab instructions and hence they were saved from being destroyed by the King of Jericho during their spying mission. One, they were told to go to the hills and secondly, they were to hide there for three days. Although the spies had witnessed God fighting their battles as they came from Egypt, they obeyed Rahab's instructions, amidst a culture where women were not highly esteemed.

Red Scarlet Chord during pandemic

The Red Scarlet Chord is the north star to be followed during the COVID-19 pandemic. From a psychological point of view, Covid-19 is likely to trigger several health challenges. The lockdown, understandably needed, has caused many losses ranging from economic, physical, to emotional losses. Sadly, companies have had to cut salary of their employees while other people have been sent on unpaid leave. Others have lost their jobs. After closing of business, the struggle of small and medium traders in trying to gather initial capital to inject into their business will be felt.

Emotional losses have also been there because of social distancing. Whereas social distancing is crucial for slowing the spread of COVID-19 virus, it affects the sense of community (ubuntu) and the support systems esteemed in many African countries. Think for example, what does it mean to work from home? How is it to be confined to your home, day in and day out, with limitations of interactions with your colleagues, neighbors and that catch-up tea or coffee dates?

Moreover, COVID-10 brings another dynamic of being limited to seeking medical services or home visits for the sick, especially the elderly- whom we value. The worst-case scenario where the ubuntu spirit is affected adversely, is when death comes knocking on the door. With the banning of public gatherings, the practice of mashakaya is affected (visits made to the deceased family during the mourning period). Ceremonies or traditions are perceived to play a major role in after-death experience. They are interpreted as a way of honoring the deceased. They also provide emotional support to those grieving while bringing family, friends, and community together to bid farewell to those who have died. They bring some sense of closure.

However, to avoid community transmission of COVID-19, burial ceremonies are restricted to one hour, regardless of whether it is COVID-19 related or not. With 1-hour window of burial, the after-death ceremonies/ traditions, like church services and speeches, are curtailed. Mourners (mainly constituting of a few 15 family members), are required to observe those regulations, besides the handwashing and sanitization. for the requirements heighten for burials of COVID-19 victims—when it comes to placing the body in the grave, gloves should be worn and once the burial is complete, hands should be washed thoroughly. As much as the measures are critical in combating transmission of COVID-19, this kind of treatment has the potential to make family members feel guilty, stigmatized, and traumatized by the handling of their loved one.

From the psychological point of view, COVID-19 is likely to trigger acute stress, anxiety, depression, and Post-Traumatic Stress Disorder (PSTD), amongst other mental health challenges. In view of this, the Red Scarlet Chord that we mainly need to focus on, is proactively looking for psycho-social support. Prior to COVID-19, statistics were already showing that 25% of Kenyans suffer from various type of mental health; mostly manifesting itself through physical challenges. Is there likelihood of those statistics rising in relation to COVID-19? The answer is likely to be 'yes' even if some fundamental guidelines have the potential to deflate the numbers.

Think about Rahab taking stalks of flax to cover the two spies. This woman used what was at her disposal and saved the lives of these two men, who later protected her family from the calamity that befell Jericho. The philosophy of ubuntu is distinctly African, and places heavy emphasis on 'we' as opposed to 'I' (Kenneth, et al 2018). Basically, ubuntu is about deliberate and intentional support system that basically looks out on others. Like stalks of flax, which may look so basic, looking for ways to maintain the family, neighborhood, and community support system, is one of the determinants that has the potential to play a key role in mental health outcomes during and after the COVID-19 season.

What is happening at the confinement of homes or family set up? Remember, one of the binding covenants between Rahab and the two spies was that her family members were to remain in the confinement of her home to be saved from Jericho's calamity. But I wonder what was happening inside the house as Rahab (who was a mature woman) stayed with her father, mother, and siblings. Without management of those relationships, acute stress was likely to hit that home. So, in the lockdown season and even after, family support system must be established. Realizing the tension of the lockdown system; anger, frustrations and conflicts are likely to escalate.

Family psychological flax will mainly consist of families having open forums to share their feelings, thoughts, and concerns (of course dependent on the age). But remember children also have their fears which maybe manifested in various ways like being clingy, crying a lot, bed-wetting or what may be termed as 'misbehavior'. They need a sense of security, affirmation, and love. Depending on their age, it is important to not only listen to their concerns or fears but also validate their feelings. For example, if they express fear, let them know it is normal to be fearful and you also have your own fears. Thereafter, talk about coping mechanisms to help you deal with fear or whatever emotion. Remember, it is in the context of open family forums that your children will realize and understand the need to streamline the budget and other family priorities. Ultimately, as a family unit, you will look for ways to not only cope with anxiety but jointly, explore your options in different matters affecting the family unit or individuals in that unit. That has the potential to reduce conflict and lower expectations of each family member.

Although community support systems have been shaken by COVID-19, the ubuntu philosophy reminds us that we can only succeed if we support each other. Can you imagine what could have happened if the spies did not adhere to Rahab's instructions about going to hide in the hills for three days? It also reminds us that even in the hardest moments, there is a 'hill' of hope. As much as restrictions on movements and gathering have been imposed, usage of telephone and digital media, provide channels that can be maximized to provide community support system.

Ultimately, the Red Scarlet Chord, which Rahab had to ensure that it was visible, is a call for Africans to embrace mental health services, including professional counseling/ psychosocial support. Mental Health impact by COVID-19 can only be ignored at the expense of 'losing' children, families, communities, and the nation. As much as the psychological ubuntu support system must be embraced at every level, a paradigm shift is needed. At the policy and citizen level, mental health services need to be recognized, appreciated, and made accessible like other medical services.

As long as mental health diseases continue to be stigmatized, and related services continue to be minimized we will be digging a hole that will swallow individuals, families, communities, and nations. Indeed, it simply increases stress to an already overwhelming pandemic situation - such as in the COVID-19 season!

PART 2: ADAPT

Adapting Wholeheartedly

Dr. Mary Thamari, Social Anthropologist and Development Practitioner

"There is only one way to survive and thrive when faced with circumstances out of our control and for which we are unprepared: ADAPT."
— Charles F Glassman

My grandfather lost one of his legs at the prime of his life in his 50s. For a generation that had spent time in the forest during their youth days fighting for independence, an education or a white-collar job was not an option for him. So what would a strong healthy man with 2 wives and 16 children do without the physical agility to walk and work? I came to know him after he had settled in his predicament, with a prosthetic leg and a set of well-organized daily routines that ensured he lived what seemed to be a full life. When I began paying attention to people and how they derive a sense of purpose to build resilience, I realized what an effort of adapting it may have been for my grandfather after his amputation.

The concept of 'adapting' is used to describe adjustments that are made following difficult situations. It is about making fitting changes so as to survive unstable circumstances (Jeans, Castillo, and Thomas 2016).

The COVID-19 pandemic has brought to the world a new set of norms and changes for which we need to adapt as necessary. Studies have shown that there are some characteristics or factors that promote an individual or organization's capacity to adapt to changes. Adaptive organizations have the following characteristics:

There are policy frameworks that support the institution's ability to adapt proactively

Have sufficient financial, technological, and human resources and the ability to use them flexibly and swiftly

Foster a culture of openness and fairness; are accountable for their actions, transparent in their dealings, and well received and respected within the community

Promote the development of a diverse range of proactive strategies and actions; has a culture of experimentation, learning and innovation

Use monitoring and evaluation to assess effectiveness and make changes through an ongoing process of incremental adjustments

Possess a strong but fluid organizational purpose, vision, and set of priorities

Think ahead to what the future may bring and incorporates this thinking into plans

Enables decision-making with minimum bureaucratic delays

Engages in partnerships and collaborative networks with other organizations

Has visionary champions (Adapted from Oxfam Resilient Development Framework)

Adaptive capacity of organizations is acclaimed as an important ingredient to recovering and bouncing back to health after difficult situations. From the lists of characteristics listed above, it is evident that they are attached to an organization's systems and structures. However, the strength of any organization is on its human resource—its people. What would be the characteristics of adaptive people then? How can people promote their own capacity to adapt to change or difficulties?

Dr. Brene Brown, a sociological researcher and a practicing Christian has developed the concept of 'wholehearted living' that I adopt to suggest the idea of 'adapting wholeheartedly' during times of difficult situations. Brown describes wholeheartedness as "engaging in our lives from a place of worthiness. It means cultivating the courage, compassion and connection to wake up in the morning and think, no matter what gets done and how much is left undone, I am enough. It is going to bed thinking, yes, I am perfect and vulnerable and sometimes afraid but that doesn't change the truth that I am worthy of love and belonging" (C. B. Brown, 2010). How do you adapt with a sense of worthiness and with courage when faced with risks and uncertainties such as what COVID-19 presents? Brown offers 10 guideposts to guide that I believe are useful in promoting adaptive resilience for individuals. These guideposts come in two parts: one on what an individual needs to embrace or nurture, and another on what they need to let go. Some of these guideposts overlap. Therefore, I will focus on 6 of the guideposts that are particularly relevant to adapting in this pandemic.

Cultivating Authenticity and letting go of what people think - Time of uncertainty can bring pressure to behave in a certain way. It may be to act in a manner that is 'acceptable' to people's expectations. Although we live in a social setting where ethical judgment on people's behavior by others is inevitable, in times of crisis, this can be an added burden. We are encouraged to be ourselves and not be overly worried about what others think we should be. I think this comes into sharp light in the phrase, "you should" – that is commonly peddled.

Although this phrase calls attention to obligations, it also creates pressure on unlimited expectations that are presented to us. Crisis causes uncertainty and can make people be more demanding on others. As a development worker or a pastor or civil servant ideas on what you should be doing at this point are many and not new and they can lead one to an overdrive even on activities that are not within your scope or capacity. Cultivating authenticity and letting go of what people think draws us to reflect on what is important, and what we are able to do in the circumstances - thereby helping sieve out unnecessary demands.

Cultivating Self-Compassion and Letting Go of Perfectionism

The pandemic has given us an unmatched sense of common humanity and solidarity in suffering than anything else in the recent history. Other humanitarian situations have been limited to specific geographical locations. In the current situation everyone is afflicted, everywhere. What this means is that there is broad understanding – everyone knows that we are operating within an unusual volatile season.

Therefore, each person has an opportunity to ease up and

cultivate self-compassion – to be kind to yourself even when you do not accomplish what you had planned. To accept that the sense of uncertainty is shared globally, and that you too can lessen your own expectations of perfection and certainty of plans and outcomes. Seeking perfectionism during such ambiguous and uncertain times, as this is not healthy and can lead to emotionally draining anxiety.

Cultivating Your Resilient Spirit, Letting Go of Numbing and Powerlessness

Resilience in its broad meaning refers to the ability to go through hardship and to recover and avert further risks. Brown offers five characteristics of resilient people: They are resourceful problem-solvers; they seek help when they need it, they take action and responsibility over their emotions, and they are connected with other people. On the contrary, we are encouraged to let go of the sense of powerlessness – this is what I see as wringing of hands in desperation and inaction. God has endowed us with power to rule and subdue the world as a gift of responsibility over everything including our emotions, actions, thoughts and decisions. Often times, people indulge in numbing activities to shake off responsibility or as an act of avoidance. Numbing activities may include workaholism, regular checks on social media, impulsive drinking of alcohol (even tea) or over eating. These numbing activities take away resilient spirit because they make one feel helpless.

Cultivating Gratitude and Joy, Letting go of Scarcity and Fear of the Dark

I was writing this morning after the organization I worked for resolved to review HR management and salaries in reference to changes in work plans and reduced funding due to COVID-19 situation. I knew this had implications on my team and their families. My mind had begun to create scenarios of what that would mean to my team, anxious thoughts began creeping on me. Realizing what I was getting into in my 'little pity party, my husband calmly stated, "we will be grateful for what we have now and not let this moment be taken away by stuff we cannot control." That did it for me – that the best way to silence fear of lack is to embrace gratitude. It is better to make decisions and take actions with an attitude of gratitude and not in fear. We cannot postpone joy in fear of something that we imagine may take that joy away.

Cultivating Intuition and Trusting Faith, Letting Go of the Need for Certainty

Human beings are wired with a yearning for certainty and inclination to take control. But COVID-19 has made a fool of our neat plans. How timely then can this be to cultivate trusting faith and to let go of need for certainty? Having learnt that there is only so much we can control in the circumstances, we now know we cannot anchor anything in certain terms. Faith according to the bible "is the substance of things hoped for, the evidence of things not seen." (Hebrews 11: 1.) Hebrews 11 gives a list of men (and women behind the scenes) who faced hardships and unprecedented situations for which they couldn't see a solution besides just believing what had been promised to them by God. We are faced with similar situation and we can begin to dream for a better post-COVID time and commit that to God.

Cultivating Play and Rest, Letting Go of Exhaustion as a Status Symbol and Productivity as Self-Worth

Even before COVID-19, norm of 'busyness' had become a symbol of pride. To rest or not to 'be busy' signaled laziness, or worthlessness. Then when the pandemic brought a related norm of virtual meetings, working from home and frenzied adjustments that became the new symbol of significance. People began listing number of zooms they do per day as a symbol of relevance. Others flaunting their ability to do it all – do housework, teach children, and still attend virtual work meetings.

Understandably, people's attempts to take control of whatever it is in their sphere of influence and these new habits create a sense of stability. Yet, these very attempts take an important basic need for rest, leading to mental overload and physical exhaustion. We are encouraged to cultivate play and rest. Unlike work, play eases up tension and even frees the mind to be more creative and imaginative. Stuart Brown, the author of Play (S. L. Brown and Vaughan 2010) argues that "the opposite of play is not work, the opposite of play is depression." Dr. Mark Shaw a Theologian and missionary who served in Africa Inland Mission (AIM) for years wrote an insightful book Work, Play, Love (Shaw 2014). He says that we need to have an integrated wholeness of life as people of God - to be free from seeking our worth and identity from work or play or love alone. To delight in whomever we work with, whatever we do and wherever we work.

These guideposts are not points of achievement but values to pursue and aim towards to help one navigate a pandemic, and life more generally.

In the chapters that follow, a clearer picture has been painted on how to support children to adapt and grow resilience, with fun and faith; to stop anxiety pandemic; to adapt to new family traditions; how men locked at home can embrace courage and care; and how to anchor our faith and hope in Christ as we adapt to confront unstable circumstances.

REFERENCES

Brown, C. Brené. 2010. The Gifts of Imperfection: Let Go of Who You Think You're Supposed to Be and Embrace Who You Are. Center City, Minn: Hazelden.

Brown, Stuart L., and Christopher C. Vaughan. 2010. Play: How It Shapes the Brain, Opens the Imagination, and Invigorates the Soul. 1. paperback ed. New York: Avery.

Jeans, H, G Castillo, and S Thomas. 2016. "The Future Is a Choice: The Oxfam Framework and Guidance for Resilient Development." http://policy-practice.oxfam.org.uk for-resilient-developme-604990.

Shaw, Mark. 2014. Work, Play, Love: A Visual Guide to Calling, Career, & the Mission of God. Downers Grove, Illinois: IVP Books, an imprint of InterVarsity Press.

Enhancing Children's Resilience During COVID-19 Pandemic

By Dr Roseline Olumbe, Holistic Child Development Expert, Daystar University

Introduction

Resilience is the capacity to function well and cope in life after exposure to adversity that threatens the normal functioning of an individual. Broadly, it refers to the capacity of a system to adapt successfully to the disturbances that threaten its stability, viability, or development (Masten 2014). This evidences that resilience can best be manifested in the context of adversity. Ungar (2018) established that there are seven principles as far as resilience is concerned. These include: (1) resilience occurs in contexts of adversity; (2) resilience is a process; (3) there are trade-offs between systems when a system experiences resilience; (4) a resilient system is open, dynamic, and complex; (5) a resilient system promotes connectivity; (6) a resilient system demonstrates experimentation and learning; and (7) a resilient system includes diversity, redundancy, and participation (Ungar 2018). As such, we cannot discuss the issue of resilience without the existence of an adversity.

Corona Virus Disease 19 (COVID-19) is highly transmittable and pathogenic viral infection which emerged in Wuhan, China in 2019 and has spread to most of the nations of the world (Shereen et al. 2020). On March 11, 2020, COVD-19 outbreak was declared a global pandemic by the World Health Organization (WHO) (Cucinotta and Vanelli 2020). This pandemic has brought about global crisis as people face a myriad of challenges such as health, economic, social, emotional and spiritual. These multiple challenges have a cumulative effect on the mental wellness of both children and adults. This paper, however, seeks to discuss the effect of these challenges on children and how parents and caregivers can inspire hope in children, thus boosting their resilience and coping mechanism.

Challenges Related to COVID-19 Pandemic on Children

COVID-19 is a health pandemic affecting the respiratory system. The patients experience flu signs including: fever, dry cough, tiredness, sore throat, and difficulty breathing. This in itself interferes with the normal functioning of the infected person. Additionally, it is noted that this virus is transmitted easily through close contact with an infected person (Shereen et al. 2020) and thus when a member of the family is infected the rest are likely to be infected. This means, that the virus is likely to affect all members of the family, leaving them devastated. Children thus may experience the physical pain, if infected by the Virus or if members of the family are infected and there is need for isolation.

The pandemic has a major socio-economic impact to diverse populations. This pandemic is evidently a human, economic and social crisis (United Nations 2020) as many parents and caregivers have lost their jobs, closed business, or lost their avenues for daily income. This has a ripple effect on the household livelihoods which affects access to food and other essential services due to loss on incomes. Children in this context are suffering the pain of hunger, loss of shelter, and lack of access to essential services. As a result, children have been deprived of their rights to survival, development, and in some cases protection and participation.

Socially, children have been deprived children of their friends and social spaces where they engage in play and recreation as the requirements for social distancing are enforced. Many children are locked up in houses as parents attempt to keep them safe from the outside space that is a threat to their wellbeing. As parents abide with the rule of social distancing, some children are exposed to social media as their point of interaction and this can be a threat to their safety especially with cybercrimes. The need to stay at home has further deprived children of opportunities to play and exercise which deprives them of physical exercise that is essential for their motor development and enhanced mental wellness.

These physical, economic and social challenges if not well mitigated could lead to emotional stress. The abrupt closure of schools and unpredictability of the future is a major concern to children. Staying indoors is a stress factor for children and can have cumulative effect on their general wellness. Parents and caregivers have a responsibility to watch for out for children's complaints, such as, somatic illness (complaints of pains in different parts of the body), persistent flu, lack of interest in play, aggression, temper tantrums, and withdrawal, anxieties, and fears among others. Lack of timely intervention could lead to toxic stress which could lead to depression and other related challenges. In order to mitigate this, parental support to children is necessary for enhanced resilience and coping.

Theories/Models of Resilience
Resiliency Theory provides a conceptual framework for

considering a strengths-based approach to understanding child and adolescent development and informing intervention design (Fergus & Zimmerman, 2005; Zimmerman & Brenner, 2010). The two commonly used resilience models are the compensatory and protective models (Fergus & Zimmerman, 2005; Garmezy, Masten, & Tellegen, 1984; Masten et al., 2007). The pictorial presentation of these models is presented in Figure 1 with compensatory model on the left and protective model on the right.

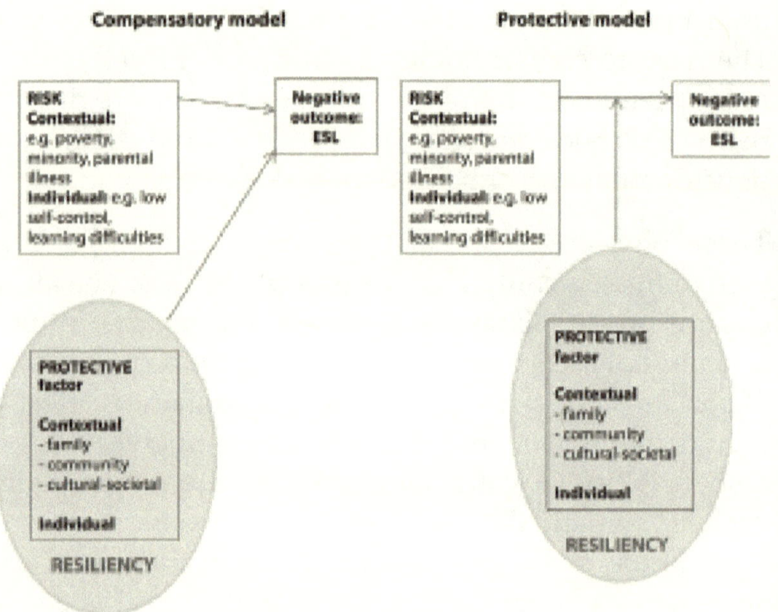

Figure 1: Compensatory and Protective Models of Resilience

Source: https://www.pei.si/ISBN/978-961-270-284-7/files/downloads/pages/Page146.pdf

Compensatory Model

Compensatory model describes the way a promotive factor counteracts or operates in the opposite direction to mitigate a risk factor (Worsley n.d.). This model indicates that the promotive factors neutralize exposure to risk and counters its effects on the individual. Promotive factors include elements like parental support which help to mitigate against fighting and being around violent adults (Zimmerman, Steinman, and Rowe 1998). In the COVID-19 context, it is assumed that if parents and caregivers are equipped to help nurture and support their children in the midst of the crisis, there will be reduction of risk factors and eventually increase in the resilience of children.

Protective Model

Protective factor models describe how assets and resources moderate or reduce the effects of a risk on a negative outcome (Worsley n.d.). Furthermore, the protective factor model holds the view that "promotive assets or resources modify the relationship between a risk, another promotive factor and outcomes" (Zimmerman 2013). The resources and assets must be adequately leveraged for positive outcomes. Resources are external factors such parental support, adult mentors programs that provide young people with opportunities to learn and practice skills, school, community, and peers. However, assets are internal and reside within an individual and they include: cooperation, empathy, problem solving, self-awareness, self-efficacy, self-esteem, goals and aspirations (Worsley, n.d.; Zimmerman, 2013). Parents and caregivers need to be aware of these assets in their children and leverage on them as they support their children to cope.

The protective model encompasses two approaches: risk-protective and protective-protective. The former implies that promotive factors act on the risk to reduce its effects and the associated negative outcomes. However, the latter works on the premise that one should enhance either of the promotive factors to increase its positive impact on the child. The protective model is relevant in the COVID-19 pandemic crisis as both approaches are helpful in increasing the resilience of a child. Parents and caregivers have a responsibility to understand this pandemic and in turn support their children to understand and cope well. By parents and caregivers explaining to children the facts of the pandemic and assuring the children that abiding by the government rules, which include: staying home, keeping social distance, and observing hygiene such as washing hands with soap or sanitizing; we are likely to reduce the spread of the virus. For this to be effectively achieved, experts in this COVID-19 need to educate parents and caregivers, but also provide best environments for parents and caregivers to thrive. As a result, the support offered to parents and caregivers will trickle to children and enhance their resilience as shown in Figure 2.

Figure 2: Increased Protective Factors for Enhanced Positive Outcomes

Source: https://www.parentingforbrain.com/resilience/

Practical Ways to Support Children in the Context of COVID-19 Pandemic

The COVID-19 pandemic has changed lives, livelihoods and lifestyles and as a result calls for a shift in our way of thinking and doing things. Individuals and families need to adopt a new way of thinking and also adapt to the shifting perspectives. The pandemic has disrupted children's education, social arenas, emotional stability and spiritual nourishment. Parents and caregivers must intervene in these changes and help children attain normalcy and adapt to the new norms of life. This paper proposes an adaptation of the STOP Sign Model, which incorporates the promotive factors for enhanced resilience in children who have experienced trauma. STOP is an abbreviation which represents the following activities to help children cope: S = Structure; T = Talk and Time; O = Organized Play; and P = Parental Support (Kilbourn 2013). Parents and caregivers should practically provide the following to their children:

Structure

COVID-19 pandemic has disrupted daily activities for children and families; and there is need to provide a structure for children so that they can function well. Provision of a structure helps children regain a sense of being in control of their situations, feelings and reactions (Kilbourn 2013). Practically, this can be done by parents and caregivers restoring a lost structure or setting in one for children. There should be a predictable routine in the home but also planned activities for children to engage. These could include: study time, play time, house chores, and rest and recreation. A clear schedule for these activities is essential and the parents and caregivers should effectively monitor to ensure children wake up to a planned and organized day. Lack of structure may leads to stress and distress and children could engage in negative activities.

A good structure is characterized by consistency, predictability and follow-through. Consistency entails setting clear activities, rules and consequences which must be adhered to leading to stability in the home. Predictability requires parents to ensure they respond in the same way to a child's behavior and this will help in emotion regulation. Additionally, children should be able to predict the next activity since it is embedded in their daily activities; and need to know what will happen if they behave in manner that is not acceptable. Finally, follow-through requires parents enforce the consequences for actions done or not done, but also establish if activities were done as required. Evidently, structure that helps children to behave entails routines and rules that are "consistent, predictable, and have a follow through" (Centers for Disease Control and Prevention [CDC], 2019).

Talk and Time

Talking is the starting point of healing process especially for children who are experiencing some level of trauma. Parents and caregivers should allow children to express their feelings which, in turn will help them become stronger, resilient, secure, feeling valued, loved and loving others. Children need time to open up, trust and be listened to as they express their feelings and concerns (Wright 2013). Parents and caregivers need to create time and listen to children either in a scheduled time or spontaneously as children play. There is need to actively listen to children by being quiet, maintaining eye-contact, and staying close.

Organized Play

Play is critical in the child's development. It is a language through which children communicate. Kilbourn (2013) notes that play is a child's natural method of learning, developing and expressing feelings. In this critical time, parents should create avenues for children to play and observe ways in which children could be expressing distress. A healthy child always plays well, however, the converse is true and one is likely to observe children who become aggressive or are not interested in play at all. In case parents or caregivers notice distress in a child, they should seek professional help. This can be done by calling Childline Kenya (a national child helpline) on their toll-free number 116 for counseling and support.

Child-centered play helps children to recapture their sense of control, power, safety, trust in adults, and hope (Heard 2013). In order to reduce pressure on children and unexpressed emotions, parents and caregivers need to organize play sessions for children within the house or outside where it is safe and secure. Parents and caregivers should provide children with safe space to play; opportunity to play; and things to play with at home (Wright 2013). Creativity is necessary to avoid high expenses and thus use locally available play materials for children to use while playing.

Parental Support

Parents have a godly task to take care of their children and support them towards healthy development. Consequently, children are wholly dependent on parental support for bonding and attachment which enables them to thrive. Although at the moment, many parents are fairly overwhelmed playing several roles and facing uncertain future, they should provide support by:

Caring for their children in a loving and trusting environment.

Parents and caregivers need to provide child friendly space for children at home so as to help them cope with the adversities. A warm environment enhances feelings of safety, security and stability. Parents and caregivers need to create this environment by demonstrating their affection and love for their children through praise, affirmation, smiles of approval and responsive to children's needs.

Meet the physical, emotional and spiritual needs of their children.

Children's physical needs include: nutritious food, clean water, shelter, clothing, exercise, healthcare and safe environment. These need to be provided adequately for children to thrive. Although many families are experiencing lockdown and staying at home, parents and caregivers need to plan for physical activities in or outside the house within supervised space. Some physical activities may include: jogging, skipping rope, walking, aerobics among others. Emotionally, parents and caregivers need to talk to their children and encourage them when overwhelmed. Spiritually, children should be allowed to engage in their faith activities such as prayer, reading/studying the Bible, singing, having home fellowship, among other faith activities despite the closure of places for worship. It is notable that spirituality is a foundation for resilience in times of adversity. As such spiritual activities must not be stopped since they are protective factors that enhance hope and resilience in children.

Make time for children and use it well.

Parents and caregivers should display interest in children's work and activities by creating time to talk or engaging in children's activities. Proactively listen to what children might say or not say so as to provide support. During this time, parents can play, talk, and even have fun with their children.

Help children solve their social, emotional and educational problems: Children may be having many questions about changes that are in place. They may want to know why they cannot visit or go and play with their friends; when schools will re-open, why they should wear masks, why they should always sanitize among others. There is need to support children and help them cope in the midst of these challenges.

Lay a proper moral and spiritual foundation for their children while promoting good discipline and character: Provide age appropriate information to children and use simple illustrations so that children can understand.

Reinforce and enforce the hygienic behavior, social distance, and stay home guidelines as guided by the government.

Develop and consistently follow a clear schedule with appropriate activities for children to engage so that they stabilize and avoid boredom which could lead them to engage in negative activities. A sample daily schedule could be as shown in Table 1. However, it should be noted that this may vary depending on one's context and age of child, hence need for adaptation.

Time	Activity	Comment
7:00 – 8:00 am	Wake up, take breakfast & freshen up	
8:00 – 9:00 am	Study	
9:00 – 9:30 am	Play/Relax/	

Time	Activity	
9:30 – 10:30 am	Study	
10:30 – 11:00 am	Play/Relax/Snack	
11:00 – 12:00 am	Study	
12:00 – 1:00 pm	House chores (cleaning, cooking, tidying etc.)	
1:00 – 2:00 pm	Lunch and Relaxation	
2:00 – 3:00 pm	Study/Read a novel	
3:00 – 4:00 pm	Watch cartoon (if possible) / read a novel/nap	
4:00 – 6:00 pm	Walk/play outside the house	
6:00 – 7:00 pm	House chores (cooking, cleaning) and bathing	
7:00 – 8:00 pm	Dinner	
8:00 – 9:00 pm	Family fun time and relaxation	
9:00pm	Retire for the day	

Table 1. Sample Daily Schedule

Conclusion

COVID-19 has a myriad of effects on children. Unless mitigated, children are likely to undergo psychological and social stress which would in turn affect their mental wellbeing. In order to mitigate this challenge and help children cope adequately, the internal and external factors must be scaffolded to help children cope. Ultimately, promotive factors must be adequately available for children to enhance their resilience. Children should be provided with supportive adult-child relationships, learning experiences that promote a sense of self-efficacy and control, life-skills that will enhance their self-regulation, and parents should use spiritual resources and family traditions as a foundation for hope and stability.

REFERENCE LIST

Cucinotta, Domenico, and Maurizio Vanelli. 2020. 'WHO Declares COVID-19 a Pandemic'. Acta Bio-Medica: Atenei Parmensis 91 (1): 157–60. https://doi.org/10.23750/abm.v91i1.9397.

Fergus, Stevenson, and Marc A. Zimmerman. 2005. 'Adolescent Resilience: A Framework for Understanding Healthy Development in the Face of Risk'. Annual Review of Public Health 26: 399–419. https://doi.org/10.1146/annurev.publhealth.26.021304.144357.

Garmezy, Norman, Ann. S. Masten, and Auke. Tellegen. 1984. 'The Study of Stress and Competence in Children: A Building Block for Developmental Psychopathology'. Child Development 55 (1): 97–111.

Heard, Mickie. 2013. '"O" Equals Organized Play: A Necessary Method for Helping and Healing'. In Healing the Children of War: A Handbook for Ministry to Children Who Have Suffered Deep Traumas, edited by Phyllis Kilbourn, 175–96. Monrovia, Calif: Wcl 3rd Party.

Kilbourn, Phyllis. 2013. 'An Introduction to the STOP Sign Model'. In Healing the Children of War: A Handbook for Ministry to Children Who Have Suffered Deep Traumas, edited by Phyllis Kilbourn, 133–46. Monrovia, Calif: Wcl 3rd Party.

Masten, Ann S. 2014. 'Global Perspectives on Resilience in Children and Youth'. Child Development 85 (1): 6–20. https://doi.org/10.1111/cdev.12205.

Masten, Ann S., J. J. Cutuli, Janette E. Herbers, and Marie-Gabrielle J. Reed. 2007. 'Resilience in Development', July. http://www.oxfordhandbooks.com/view/10.1093/oxfordhb/9780195187243.001.0001/oxfordhb-9780195187243-e-012.

Shereen, Muhammad Adnan, Suliman Khan, Abeer Kazmi, Nadia Bashir, and Rabeea Siddique. 2020. 'COVID-19

Infection: Origin, Transmission, and Characteristics of Human Coronaviruses'. Journal of Advanced Research 24 (July): 91–98. https://doi.org/10.1016/j.jare.2020.03.005.

Ungar, Michael. 2018. 'Systemic Resilience: Principles and Processes for a Science of Change in Contexts of Adversity'. Ecology and Society 23 (4). https://doi.org/10.5751/ES-10385-230434.

United Nations. 2020. 'The Social Impact of COVID-19'. DISD. 2020. https://www.un.org/development/desa/dspd/2020/04/social-impact-of-covid-19/.

Worsley, Lyn. n.d. 'The Resilience Doughnut Model: A Model Showing the Interaction of External Resources That Build Individual Resilience'. Alpha Psychology and the Resilience Centre; and The Resilience Doughnut PTY Ltd. Accessed 18 April 2020. https://www.resiliencereport.com/var/file/research/The%20resilience%20doughnut%20general%20paper.pdf.

Wright, Josephine. 2013. '"T" Equals Talk and Time: Reaching the Troubled or Traumatized Child'. In Healing the Children of War: A Handbook for Ministry to Children Who Have Suffered Deep Traumas, edited by Phyllis Kilbourn, 157–74. Monrovia, Calif: Wcl 3rd Party.

Zimmerman, Marc A. 2013. 'Resiliency Theory: A Strengths-Based Approach to Research and Practice for Adolescent Health'. Health Education & Behavior : The Official Publication of the Society for Public Health Education 40 (4): 381–83. https://doi.org/10.1177/1090198113493782.

Zimmerman, Marc A., Kenneth J. Steinman, and Karen J. Rowe. 1998. 'Violence among Urban African American Adolescents: The Protective Effects of Parental Support'. In Addressing Community Problems: Psychological Research and Interventions, edited by X. B. Arriaga and S. Oskamp, 78–103. The Clarement Symposium on Applied Social Psychology. Thousand Oaks, CA, US: Sage Publications, Inc.

Parenting: Fun, Faith & Fortitude.

By Angela Obwaka, Human Resources Consultant and Faith Vlogger

I do not consider myself a perfect parent. I'm not sure anyone does. And in as much as we would agree about this, we tend to measure ourselves against some standard of perfection that is impossible to attain save for God's parenting. This season more than most, brings out this pressure to be and do so much than we have prepared for and quite frankly, without a plan or guide – it can feel overwhelming. So you are not alone. As a popular song from high school musical goes, "We are all in this together".

As an individual, I believe I am called to demonstrate to my children what abandonment in love, worship and pursuit of Jesus looks like. So because of that, I am very open and vulnerable with my life both with my children and with the world—because how can they know how AWESOME Jesus is if they only see JESUS relating with the 'perfect', or put-together or always proper ones? Jesus Himself said: "I did not come to save the righteous, I came to seek and SAVE the lost." This, He said in the house of a tax collector, one who was considered not worthy of Jesus' visit.

In my parenting, I want my children to know the following:

1. To know God cares by how He cares for me

2. To know that He answers prayer by journeying

with me through my prayers

3. To know that His Word is true by standing on His promises along with them

Children need to be invited behind the curtain to see 'where the magic happens' with your own relationship with God. They need to see beyond Sunday and beyond daily devotions. Here are my 6 ideas for building faith and fortitude.

Demonstrating God's goodness and kindness

Ensure your kids know that they are not a bother – not a burden – not a kill joy or a distraction. Research shows that our children get ideas about who God is from their parents or parental figures. If we are going to be modeling Christ and God's love, they need to know they are loved and wanted. That their presence is valuable and not an inconvenience. That their worldview is unique and not childish or stupid. That their voice and contribution matters. So, if they suggest different ways of doing things, let them explain their processing, offer solutions etc. The kindness usually reserved for work colleagues, cell group members and pastors? You get to serve that to your kids. Do it as unto the Lord whether they notice it or not.

Action Points:

*   Pray for yourself each morning before you engage with the kids (as part of your devotions). Pray for joy, for patience and pray to ENJOY your kids and to treat them with kindness.
*   Daily let them know that you are glad you have them and glad you are getting to spend time together.

Model trust and dependence on God

Children are so much smarter than adults often. Give them credit for and despite the face you are putting on for them, they are picking up on your hoarding, secret anxious conversations, and criticism of the government, neighbors, church leaders as well as gossip and complaining sessions.

Although we are all wondering about when this season will end, we don't need to be or making negative comments every 2 minutes. This usually happens in private or as part of 'regular day' conversation and then in the evening or during family devotions, there is a separate more faith-sounding request shared. Children are not served well by your pretense. If anything, they will likely pick up that God wants a particular type of façade rather than the truth about what is going on and that will hinder their connection with Him now and later.

Action Point: How about we being vulnerable with our kids about concerns we each have and then together present them to the Lord?

Personal Testimony: I recently shared a concern with my kids about rent. Not that I was worried we would be thrown out but asking God to provide the rent in totality by the end of the month in light of economic shifts, and He did. The kids (well mostly my 11-year old), went wild because he knew I was serious when I was sharing the request and how much this was a concern to me in my human limitations.

Sharing God's Perspective

COVID-19 is a reality with us and we are not going to shelter our kids from the reality of life. However, we can teach them to process life through the reality of who

God is and His Word. Yes, covid-19 is here. Yes, people are dying from it. Yes, people are losing their jobs. But that's not where it ends. Just yesterday I was reflecting on the statement everyone keeps making "Everywhere you look, it's just bad news…the media is full of bad news…" Then I thought to myself - this is only a problem if you are hoping for good news from there. But guess what, we already have the good news found in the Bible. The good news is in the person of Jesus Christ and connection to a good father.

So let's see what He says: Philippians 4:6-7: Pray about everything.

- My kids and I developed a prayer chart from manilla paper with 1 Timothy 2:1-4 written out on the top and then we listed various prayer needs on it. During prayer time we asked the questions: who do you think needs help? Who needs wisdom? Who can we pray for? Who needs a job? This ranges from health care workers, government, ministry of health etc.

- Then we cut up little strips of paper, wrote those same names on the pieces of paper, folded them and put them in a little bag. Every night, we have devotions and an opportunity to pick out two (or more) names from the personal bag and we pray about their needs and then put them back.

- This helps the kids know they can EFFECT change with just their prayers, build their FAITH when prayers get answered and KNOW that God cares about all the big and small things as perceived and presented by His children.

Ideas for Parenting with Fun

1. Investigative Assignments

There are also really good ideas to engage kids with in this season. There are a lot of things happening and unless we take time to intentionally process them with our children, they will remain floating about in their minds, only to be resolved by non-Biblical sources. Some of these on things related to COVID-19 include:

- Is God good?
- Did God cause the Coronavirus?
- If God is so powerful, how come He's not stopping it?
- God our Healer – What does healing look like?
- What happens when we die?

These can be spread out over a week/weeks and you and kids can investigate key stories (story of Joseph, story of Moses (and the babies being thrown into the Nile) using the bible. Use pictures to present, Internet to research, and other books.

2. Sharing daily highlight and lowlights

At meal times or devotions, these questions can open up sharing:

- What are you thankful for today

- What happened in your day today that made you encouraged, excited or filled up your cup with love from God?

- What are you struggling with that we can pray for?

The responses need to be specific in their sharing. Not sharing 'I'm grateful for life', even if they are. This helps keep everyone thankful and see God's involvement in tiny ways in our day and helps us check-in genuinely on what they could be processing in this season. The cabin fever, lack of external connection could be weighing down on them and we don't want to miss it.

3. **Other activities you can do together**

- Daily family devotions
- Memorizing scripture
- Treasure hunts based on stories you have read or are reading together in the bible.

Bible crafts: Here https://www.crossway.org/books/the-big-picture-bible-crafts-tpb/ by Gail Schoonmaker courtesy of Crossway offers 101 simple and amazing crafts to help teach children the Bible.

THE END! These are MANY options – you don't have to do EVERY single one of them but you also don't have to struggle trying to figure out how to point them to Jesus and DISCIPLE them in this season. May they love Jesus more, be more open to prayer, His Word, and even salvation out of being stuck with you during this pandemic!

Restoring Family to the Core of Community

By Pastor David Ewagata, Director of YHub NetworX

The earth is breathing; shouldn't our homes breath too?

A number of spectacular pictures have come up of our beautiful mountains being spotted from our balconies in the city. Apparently, the earth is breathing for the lack of smog and smoke and greenhouse gases and we can see the peak of Mt. Kilimanjaro from the peak of Mount Kenya (Sic). Speed, performance, and presence for everything and everyone else has been the mantra for the city. We have drowned nature in the process. A buck here, a buck there has been the motivation for every living human. If you are not number one, you are not it. The chase for the mighty dollar has characterized our living, loving, doing, and being.

However, I want to zero in on the home. That is where most of us are stuck right now with Covid-19 restrictions. We are not stuck in the office with our dear paper files. We are not stuck at school with our dear teacher. We are not stuck in our politicians' compounds receiving handouts, empty rhetoric, and ridiculous promises. No! We are all stuck at home. We are stuck with the people we were raised with, the people we married, the people we are raising, or the people we want to share our loots and spoils of life with. So, the home must be of great interest.

We sent our children to school and assumed the role of long-distance parents if not a totally absent one for that matter. We played ping-pong with various topics being juggled between state, church, family, and school. Sex education was hurriedly handed to the religious organizations, information dissipation handed to educational institutions, career development handed to life-coaches, mentors, personal coaches, and other loftily titled human strategists. Mental, emotional, and social adjustment issues were handed over to the counsellors. While at home, the parents only supplied food, accommodation, and the occasional pat in the back for children.

Here are 5 things we must address:

Escape: Our natural default

The largest amount of time in all of life has been spent plotting the grand escape. We know how that works. You have a good job, you have a perfect alibi. You have to travel, you have to see new clients, you have to have the report ready. Deadlines. Deadlines. Deadlines. Every time something needs attention, you beat it back with an expensive gift, an exotic holiday, or just sheer avoidance. Many of us were simply renting out children- to school, to the TV, to church (Sunday school teacher/youth pastor). Now we are parenting. We thought we were parenting but now we realize we were on cruise control, safe-mode, autopilot, remote control, and any other option - all except full-on parenting.

Most of us were dating our jobs, hiding in the traffic jam, attending MBA classes after work, now we are truly married! In fact, most couples have not been this together since they got married and joined the rat race. Some of those with global positions have never been on the ground this long.

We had totally structured, compartmentalized,

department-alized and professionalized all our roles as regarding marriage and family. If you want to know which part of your life is most tended, see where most progress is made. Our careers have never been that efficient. Our services to others are impeccable, but our homes? They have been the subjects of neglect. By some providence, God has seen it fit to restructure our compartmentalized lives into one bucket - home! Everything is localized within the home: Learning, work, entertainment, sports, faith, and socialization. We must stop and pay attention to the home, for there is no more escape.

Endure

This is the crux of the matter. It will be painful before it becomes pleasant. It is like stepping into the gym by force and for the first time. The first days seem to be murder - to put it mildly. Many people throw in the towel just when they should have pressed on a bit. Many families are under duress. The father is home constantly. They were okay with him being there for the sporadic moments and had learnt to sneak to the bedroom or kitchen the moment he walks in. They spoke in hushed tones till he left again to go hang out with his crew because he was equally uncomfortable. He would leave and they would walk back to the living room, throw their good selves on the seats and enjoy his DSTV, food, and accommodation. But now in Covid-19 times, he is here, he is there, he is still here, he is staring at you wondering what you do with your life. He is wondering why it takes 3 people so long to make a meal every day. He is asking or worse still, he is just silently watching, getting angry, or getting restless.

At this moment we have a choice. To keep truce till Coronavirus leaves, or to move a muscle in an attempt to restore community, and hope to live to tell the story.

As I said earlier, it is not easy and it won't be easy! Many have lived in a marital cul-de-sac for years- its been truce rather than love that bound us together. It is cued into our systems. It's in our neuropaths. It's our precious normal. We don't like it, but we have never had to deal with it. This must lend itself to the next step.

Engage

Many would want to stave off the need to actually make the necessary changes because, let's face it, it's difficult to engage when years have passed without any much interaction. We must take the scary but necessary step to start off what we left off during our dating days. Marriage long became a certificate, a longevity of stay in the same abode, and the exchange of sporadic pleasantries, delegation of certain duties, and the meeting of a variety of obligations.

In reality, marriage became the butt of all jokes on how boring and bogus it is. It is seen as a necessary burden full of woes unending. Instead of working on our marriages, we invested in other more exciting prospects and relationships, only to be stuck with, yes, family! Why? Because when all is said and done, these are the very people who really, really matter.

With this knowledge in mind, we must ask ourselves what it will take to restore our relationships back to where they were. This may be the space of time to do it. You see, nobody marries the wrong person; we simply wrong the right person. Here we are with a window to right the wrong. If we know just how much more important this is to the wellbeing of our children as compared to any other provision we work hard to offer, we will stop gladly and shift priorities drastically. Many of our children's drug problems, mental health issues, deviant behaviours, and moral vices stem from our failures at home- not at work or in the community. We can never build a healthy nation on the backbone of an unhealthy home.

Engrave

One of my favourite bosses of all time used to love making this statement: "Paths are made by walking." Every time we faced a new challenge that had no precedence, he would pull up this statement and start us off on a journey of beating out a new path. The joy of this venture is gripped with the fear of the same. It's a new canvas, a blank page, a new beginning. On the flip side, it is the stuff of analysis paralysis, paralysis of a blank page, the fear of the unknown, and the stress of the only constant in life- Change! If we can form new patterns after this season, if we can replace old ways of doing things during this season, if we can change our priorities in this season, we can actually set the entire world in a new trajectory. Life as we know it will never be the same.

Once healthy patterns are put in place, how I pray that they will be engraved in the lives of our families. May we not go back to cheap communication, rabid schedules, and old ways of doing family. May the end of Covid-19 not be the end of our healthy regiments!

Enjoy

If we take this process to the end, we shall then be able to stand on the other side and celebrate a whole new world. There are many, many pertinent things that need to change in our society and Covid-19 is possibly the least of our worries though it's right now the talk on everyone's lips. It's like a new toy- the new kid on the block. It has made HIV, Ebola, Sars, Malaria, Cancer, et.al take a respectful back seat! However, if victory over Covid-19 is our only victory after this is all said and done, we have lost the greatest battle! Covid-19 has given an opportunity to do what all our leave days, all our holidays, and all our sick leave days would not do for the entire world. The world is breathing, shouldn't we?

The earth is breathing, shouldn't our homes breath too?

How to Stop the Anxiety Pandemic

By Christi A. Byerly, PCC, SD, Spiritual Alignment Coach

Anxiety is the most contagious emotion: I lived in Kenya for eleven years, and I used to love to leave the city of Nairobi and drive out across the plains toward Athi River, observing the herds of gazelles, zebras, and wildebeest out grazing peacefully. Content to cluster together in their community groups, the tails of the Thompson gazelles would switch lazily, and their heads were often down in the grass as they focused on their munching.

Occasionally, the entire herd, numbering well into the hundreds, would perk up in the same moment. Every head up and alert. Every heart beating rapidly. Every eye wide and focused. Every muscle tensed, the flight instinct honed to perfection.

To feel anxious is to be a part of the animal kingdom. Anxiety is human, and it runs through groups of humans in a split second. Now that the whole world is connected virtually, our human herd is collectively alert and ready to clash horns or start a stampede.

Anxiety can last a very long time in humans:
When anxiety shows up, we feel it first in our bodies. As humans, however, we also think anxiety in our heads, which is why anxiety can last so much longer with us. Not only do we feel muscle tension, and notice the heart rate going up; we also ruminate, which means thinking

about and imagining negative outcomes, especially catastrophic scenarios.

In this age of viral contagion, our thoughts easily move to such things as, "Will I lose my job, my house, my loved ones?" We are especially prone to worrying about things we can't control, things that fighting, fleeing and freezing cannot resolve. Few of the people I've talked with are actually worried about getting the virus themselves, but many of us worry a lot about the people we care about, and who we fear we can't help. For example, keeping the 70-year-olds in line is a hard job!

The human brain is capable of long-term thinking and planning (and worrying). On our best days, we can envision what we'll make for dinner, but also what kind of business revenues we would like to have in five years' time, and what kind of university degree will be best for our current three-year-old. That means that we're also capable of thinking about all the things we can lose. Some people become adept at imagining the most painful worst-case scenarios possible, and dress-rehearsing tragedies many years before their time.

Anxiety feels lonely and shameful

Unlike the animals, humans have the capability to self-isolate, and we have been forced to distance ourselves physically from one another, some of us for weeks already. So, instead of only feeling the anxiety as a herd, we can also think that we're alone and the only one who could possibly be feeling so awful. We turn to instagram, twitter and facebook for relief, but see other people's beautiful photographs of laughter, good times and how well everyone else seems to be handling things. "They" all seem to have energy to spare to share with others. CXXC XCB XCB XCB XCNB NBXB

Some of us have marching orders in our heads like, "Fear not!" or "Serenity Now" and we think that we're wrong and bad to be unable to control our emotions, which often feels like fear, anger, worry, frustration, irritation and grief, in addition to anxiety. It's easy to think that I'm the only person walking around with this undercurrent of anxiety, and easy to put a good face on it and further isolate myself. When we don't acknowledge, name and accept these feelings, they tend to rule over us, and we can find ourselves snapping at loved ones, over-functioning, micromanaging or melting down, without spending adequate time feeling what we are feeling.

So, what's the antidote to the anxiety pandemic?

Stay, stay, stay….

I've never trained a pet dog, but I know that many dogs learn the word, "Stay!" as one of their first commands. When they feel like jumping up and running away, they learn to manage the discomfort and stay in the moment. As humans, we have the benefit of our prefrontal cortex--the part of the brain that allows for thinking, and so we can tell ourselves to slow down and pay attention to the present moment.

Stay in community:

Each one of us has been loved into life. We wouldn't have made it this far if not for people around us tending to our needs and ensuring we had food, drink, touch, love and everything we needed. It's time to turn toward that well-spring of life.

Things may not be fine. I might lose my job. I might lose a loved one. But when I tell the story of my fears and hopes more truly with someone, I am more fully seen and known. There's a huge opportunity for connection, forgiveness and community. It's a practice! Every day, touch base with two or three people who you know and love. Connect, ask them how they are, and let them hear how you are doing as well.

Some of us are part of faith communities. We know ourselves to be connected to the great I AM, the source of all life. When we honestly tell who we are, and we know that we are not alone, and we hear other stories, we remember that we are not alone, and that we are a part of history that is moving toward greater faith, hope and love.

When I lived in Kenya, there was a time of fear when my fellow Americans were evacuating during a period of conflict after national elections. The day of the American evacuation, I chose to go to the plant store. I purchased passion fruit vines, and orange, apple and mango tree saplings and planted them in my garden. I chose faith over fear.

We are living in a bigger story of connection. I was born into the Judeo-Christian tradition and grew up hearing the story of Jeremiah, who was told to build houses, plant gardens and have babies in a time of exile. Do everything you can for the flourishing of the location and community where you are, and partake in a movement toward faith, hope and love.

Stay in the body

When the herd of Thompson gazelles knows that the danger is past, when the predator has moved on, you can actually see the whole herd shake it off. Each animal literally sends a visible shiver down its body. This shaking and shivering movement releases the pent-up anxious chemicals and allows the animal to go back to grazing, digesting food or sleeping in a relaxed way.

In the same way, the human body also benefits from a shaking motion. I recommend dancing with a "Five Rhythms" dance pattern of Flowing, Staccato, Chaos, Lyrical and Stillness. Even a few jumping jacks, a five-minute walk or jog, or a little hokey-pokey with the kids can do wonders. It doesn't take long to remember to literally shake it off.

Your body is beautiful and useful and powerful. It's so good to immerse ourselves every, single day in the joy of being alive right now. See what happens when you turn on joyful music you can sing along with loudly, in a standing posture if possible. You can use the body to dance and stay in motion.

I find it very grounding to use the five senses. When I feel my heart racing, I can notice four red objects in my environment, three textures I can touch, two sounds I can hear, et cetera. I can remember that staying right here, right now--I am OK.

Stay creative

In recent weeks, I started Friday creative parties with a group I lead. There's something about creativity that's so basic, and that keeps us focused and free from the fear of scarcity. A few blobs of paint turned into a landscape, an old cross-stitch pattern found in a drawer, a quilting square that's been hiding for years under the bed, a graphic design project for work... all of these are ideas the women I work with have come up with the move into a sense of agency and joy. I know that you have some creative ideas that are just waiting to happen, and that may even be of great service to the world.

Stay in the practice of gratitude

Every day, morning and night, write down three things you're grateful for. A gratitude practice is inextricably linked to joy. And it's impossible to feel fear and gratitude at the same time. So choose gratitude as a regular practice.

Stay in touch

It may be a good idea to share with someone what's helping you stay courageous and loving in these anxious times. I'd love to hear what's helping and what's blocking you from joy and kindness. You can reach out to me at christi@awakencoaching.com.

The Silence Is Broken: Embracing Hope

By Rev. Canon Francis Omondi, Priest of the Anglican Church of Kenya, of All Saints Cathedral Diocese.

Mary Magdalene, and Mary the mother of James, and Salome became more eloquent in silence than words, and we can interpret this in many ways. The day after Sabbath, of crucifixion, they slithered in the halo of silence to the tomb with choice spices to anoint Jesus's body. You may be right to think they feared. For the Galileans had become an endangered species in Jerusalem during this Passover. The lynching mobs were still in town, you would be very afraid if you had ever been associated with the man of Galilee.

The haunting voices of the crowds baying for Jesus' blood vibrated along the narrow streets of Jerusalem. For instance, a sound one makes outside appears to echo the chants: "away with this man…", "crucify him!", "we have no king, we have no king… but Ceaser", all this would ring in one's mind. How could they speak to anyone in Jerusalem without risking being lynched? In their silence, the women didn't arrange for the stone movers at the grave. And this troubled them. But how could they trust the men of their company, who themselves were silent and afraid? The men had a distinct silence, a defeated silence. Like when one can tell no more stories. Akin to what Rabbi Hugo Gryn describes when he arrived at Auschwitz—the entrance to the camp was littered with thrown away tefillin. The Jews used the tefillin in daily Jewish prayers. This became a sign that here in the camp, there was no point in praying any longer.

These men from Galilee had been sustained with a narrative on the road to Jerusalem. And they were convinced of what would happen. The Romans would be driven out at last. Jesus would restore the kingdom to Israel and be their warrior king. A similar confession was blurted out in disappointment on another road, the road to Emmaus: "we had hoped he was the one to redeem Israel." Faced with Jesus' passion and death, the disciples had no story to tell of the future. In that crisis moment, when this fragile community was disintegrating, Jesus took bread and blessed it and gave it to them saying, 'this is my body, given for you'. He gave himself them, to hold them together in their eminent scattering.

The women knew this and something else about the men that they were not to be counted on for the "operation back to the tomb". Jesus had exposed them during the last supper. That is the night Judas had sold Jesus, Peter was about to deny him, yes, Peter would betray him, and the other disciples would flee in fear. So, you get the picture on why the women were silent. In the words of Paul Simon, these women dared disturb the sound of silence. (Paul Simon 1964 Song, The Sound of Silence). The stone at the opening yielded in the naked light of the angle. And the tomb talked without speaking. The women heard without listening. They were writing songs that voices never share.

The radiant tomb broke the silence:

"Do not be alarmed. You seek Jesus of Nazareth, who was crucified. He has risen; he is not here. See the place where they laid him. But go tell his disciples and Peter that he is going before you to Galilee. There you will see him, just as he told you" (Mark 16:6-7). But the women remained silent. Why aren't the women rejoicing that Christ is risen? You wonder. Can't they see that the tomb is empty?

St. Mark entered the women's silence. See how he ends the most dramatic of the Gospels with the very brave women's silence. Mark observes, "… they went out and fled from the tomb, for trembling and astonishment had seized them, and they said nothing to anyone, for they were afraid" (Mark 16:8). He had seen a lot that weekend, enough to narrate the story from the last supper to the empty tomb. Yet he refuses to end this Gospel with an explosion of Joy at the resurrection.

The women's puzzling sound of silence spoke to Mark's readers in Rome. Mark wanted his readers to discover themselves in the silent women. The disciples in Rome had created a narrative for the future. The second coming of Christ. This hope intensified with the increase in persecution by Nero in AD 60s. Peter and Paul were murdered, the Roman Christians were filled with dismay and distrust, with betraying one another to avoid persecution, Jesus must be eminent. But he did not come.

Embracing Hope

Though Jesus was not present in the tomb, the women and his followers could still meet him, said the angel: "He is going before you to Galilee; there you will see him as he told you." Mark wished his readers embraced the women's hope and live this promise of Jesus with joy.

The silent women still speak to us who seek to find the Savior. Jesus is not in the tomb he is found in his word and in his promises, for he has gone out to Galilee. Suspending gathering in church buildings to curb the spread of coronavirus has opened us to the notion of Jesus' presence outside.

"He is not here" was the angel's counsel to the women we ought to heed. We may not meet Christ in our familiar places because he has arrived at the rendezvous, and there he is waiting for us. Jesus is locked down with the poor. He is there with those who suffer hunger because they have not been at work. Jesus is with the sick who have no healthcare. He is with those violently oppressed and made poor by structural injustices How do we whisper in silence when Jesus is already waiting for us?

Perhaps when we follow Jesus 'out there' we will find him with the poor whose rights are violated. The devastating impact of COVID 19 has exposed the façade, and we can't hide our violence on the poor. As citizens, we have an unconditional obligation to the victims of unjust society.

We may be victims of the direct or indirect injustices. We must aid such victims for we are also victims. When we follow Jesus out there, acting towards helping the invisible poor, will provide for those through this crisis lost jobs and means of living without waiting for the state to act. We must demand that the state takes its responsibility seriously. Majority of the poor Kenyans in the cities depend on casual work for day to day supply, they have not worked for weeks now and more are coming. What assurance do we have that we have food in the national reserve, and where will they get that food? It is a planting season. Who is guiding planting to provide for us food by August? Their children are with them and not in school. We just learnt that 4 million youth willing to work are unemployed. What is the government policies on the poor, unemployed and healthcare for the poor? The state has a responsibility to better lives of all Kenyans, including the poor.

Who would, but the church, to question and act on these

issues? As we arrived at the triumphant Easter, we may like the women, be locked in silence if fear has made us blind. Such fear may extinguish our glow. If the church must be a true witness for Christ in crisis time, it must find courage, the silent courage of the women that led them out.

So, every time we gather as a community to celebrate the Eucharist, we remember the moment in which Jesus faced death and disintegration when the disciples had lost what to say about where they were going. We do so with words that come from the Gospels, which were written in the light of the second significant loss of a story about the future when Jesus didn't return when they expected. The COVID-19 crisis has wrecked our characterization of Christ. It has made tombs of our church institutions, releasing Jesus into the society. Can we imagine the open tomb, with Jesus is recasting his church in the society, in families, among the suffering poor?

As this Gospel ends with the angel's initiation to carry on the journey. The end of the gospel is not the end of the story, but the beginning of the journey, our journey. The women walked it in silence. We must keep on walking our walk.

MEN @ HOME: Embracing Courage, Care and Comradeship

By Simon Mbevi. Founder and Director of Transform Nations and Man Enough

The changes that have resulted from this pandemic have caused lots of stress, at home especially. The men have struggled to cope, probably a lot more than the women. This is for several reasons:

Men usually stay less at home compared to women. More men are a lot more comfortable out there – leaving home very early and coming back late. Many men find their significance mainly in the work they do out there. Culturally and biologically men are oriented towards productive economic spaces as opposed to reproductive economic space where childcare and domestic activities are executed.

Men are less relational than women. The relationships at home – with spouse and children – can be very challenging to men with the increased number of hours spent at home. Although men and women have inherent need for connection, men are less likely to voluntarily seek supportive relationships or build connections than women. A broad scan of self-help groups and support groups indicates less membership by men.

The stress of limited activities, movement and work has hit the men pretty hard. Generally, in stressful situations, men take longer to process in their minds emotionally, talk less about their feelings and feel a lot more frustrated when they cannot fix the problems. Women on the other hand, process their emotions a lot quicker, share freely with their friends and that reduces the stress, and have more nesting instincts and developed skills than men.

The economic implications of the pandemic have affected many men negatively. Men see money as power, and when they cannot access it due to loss of job or they have reduced income, they struggle a lot more than women to cope. I usually ask men if they would be happy to marry ladies who earn a lot more than them. The answer, in three out of four men, is usually a loud "NO". Lots of men during this time feel diminished in their significance and reduced in their influence. It does not take a lot more to stress a man.

What should men do with all these challenges they are facing? Here are four suggestions especially for men but not exclusive to them – the four C's.

Courage

Men at this time need to master courage in three areas. First is moral courage, the courage to do what is right and just in their relationships at home. Crisis, like we are in, has a way of revealing the best of character and exposing the dark sides thereof. Men need to man-up to strengthen the good in them and change the bad. The courage to change is called for. For the men who have found themselves having anger management problems, this is the time to find help to deal with that. Acts of physical and emotional abuse should be discarded for what they are, acts of cowardice.

Second is courage to accept. Men need to master the courage to face the prevailing reality. To accept what they cannot change, change and improve what they can and trust God for the future. Reality reveals that we are limited as humans, and that we need the divine to survive. Men need to be courageous enough to pray and grow in their spirituality.

Lastly we need leadership courage. The courage for self-leadership – re-plan our lives, motivate ourselves, manage our time well and stay productive. We also need to courageously lead in the places where we have influence. At home we need, alongside our wives (for the married), to lead the family through these stormy times. Decisions need to be made and executed, encouragement and motivation given especially to the children, and teamwork coordinated for everyone to carry their load at home. Studies have shown that women carry triple work burdens as they take on productive roles (formal jobs), reproductive roles (child bearing and nurture) and community roles. This has been escalated by school closures adding on to this burden. As man, leadership demands your recognition of this reality and to take on some of this burden as a protection action for you spouse. Leaders generate ideas and give guidance during crisis times. The men, who are leaders at work, need the courage to lead there and navigate their teams through the season. Leaders must have the courage to make tough calls when necessary.

Care

A man shines brightest when he uses his manly power to care for others. Care is love released. Spouses need tender love during this season. Children need fatherly love. Siblings and friends need brotherly love. The weak, poor and struggling need the "Good Samaritan" love. This is the time for men to stand tall by bending furthest to pull up, hold and walk with those they care for dearly and those in need.

Men, we need to use this time to build bridges and initiate reconciliations in our relationships at home and outside the home. Real men swallow their pride and seek for forgiveness as they offer it to those who need it. Healed relationships are the taste of heaven. We need to reach out and strengthen our marriages, our parenting relationships and other friendships. Care compels us to reach out and heal relationships, especially the ones at home where we are currently spending more time than before.

Calculate

The economy is taking a beating. Cash flow has been affected. Some have lost jobs, others are struggling to keep their businesses afloat. It is a hard time financially. And this is likely to drag and get worse in the coming months. As men we need to assess our financial situation and make the right decisions. Cut costs, so that you may stretch the resources you have to last longer. Review the state of our investments, and protect or dispose of them as the realities may demand. Reduce our expenses as we face an uncertain future.

Do the math and see what next steps you need to take to survive through the crisis financially. Make the changes at work and in business as it is needed. Plan for the after Covid-19. Make calculations and do the necessary – close up business, trim the workforce, change the way you do business, find a different line of work, give generously, cushion your workers – whatever the case maybe.

Comrades.

"A friend loves at all times, and a brother is born for a time of adversity" (Proverbs 17:17) Life was meant to be lived in community. Alone is not great. The lone ranger mentality only belongs to the movies. Men are made men among men.

Man, you need to reflect on the brothers that you have. You need close men who are committed to you. Men who love you at all times – love is about a commitment to the welfare of another. Men who stand with you in times of adversity.

You need three to five men who do life with you. Men you are open and vulnerable with. Such brothers need to have a shared vision with you. Men of the same worldview and overall direction of life. Secondly, you need men of shared values. Men you share the basic convictions of life so that there is less conflict or contradiction. The Bible asks, "Can two walk together unless they agree?" (Amos 3:3) Brotherhood best works around shared core values. Lastly, you need men who are valuable to you. People you value deeply, love in your heart, are committed to and enjoy being around them.

So, the question is, Do you have such kind of brothers? If you do, this is the time to strengthen those relationships. Call them regularly during this crisis, pray together, talk about each other's feelings and struggles, stand with each other. If you don't, find them. Start the process of building such brotherhood.

Lastly, you need a man or several who can speak into your life. Truth tellers. 'Prophets' like Nathan was to king David. Respected men who can correct you and challenge you. At the same time, you need younger men that you are mentoring. Pass on the lessons you have learned in life, both in success and in failure, to a few select apprentices. Legacy is built as we raise up others. Be a father to a few young men. Pass on the baton of courageous masculinity.

Coach the un-fathered. This is a good time to call a few young men and agree on a way to walk together.

Summary.

Men @ home, we need the courage to face ourselves and the reality around us. Deep care to those who matter most to us at home and to the needy. We need to make calculations and manage our personal, family and business economies. We need comrades that we stand with during these tumultuous times.

Men, let us be the better for going through this season. Let us come out better but not bitter, refined and not raw. The lockdowns should not be an excuse to man down. Let us enjoy and exhibit the glory of masculinity. And for ladies, let us support the men as they reflect and grow on the four C's.

PART 3: ACT WITH HOPE

The Journey Within: Taking action for Mental Health

Dr. Charity Waithima, Clinical Psychologist

The recent outbreak of Severe Acute Respiratory Syndrome Coronavirus 2 (SARS-CoV-2) has put shivers in every human spine. The disease caused by a novel coronavirus, is transmitted from human to human by cough or sneeze droplets from an infected person. Everybody is at high risk as thousands of people have been infected globally. Countries were caught off guard which presented in terms of lack of awareness and preparedness, poor governmental and institutional infection control measures and lack of community training in handling the pandemic, hence poor compliance with the use of personal protection. This was complicated by other measures that had to be introduced in attempts by governments to combat the unknown health monster. Some of the measures included quarantine for all who had travelled from the so-called Covid-19 hotspots or those who had contact with those who had tested positive with the virus.

Other measures were social distancing; dusk to dawn curfews, wearing of protective gear such as masks and for the frontline workers the personal protective equipment. There were effects on many people's traditional activities

"

and routines including closure of places of worship, schools and colleges. Employees were asked to work from home, and some lost their jobs or businesses which was the source of livelihood. Containment measures were declared, families and loved ones cannot not visit each other or have their social normal. Those who lose loved ones through death can no longer have their significant others support. The taking away of social support that is known to be critical in coping with a crisis can lead to serious psychological distress or on the extreme emotional burnout. Some family members have had to miss the final rights after the death of loved ones, leaving them with unfinished business. The "stay home, stay safe" mantra is now a new common slogan. This so called the global new normal has brought the beginning of a new journey within every human being.

The fear and anxiety about an outbreak of an unfamiliar fatal disease can be overwhelming and cause strong emotions. As the corona virus pandemic rapidly sweeps across the world, no one is committal to telling people how long this situation will last. The World Health Organization (WHO) and the Center for Disease Control (CDC) have not even addressed the issue of how long we will be wearing masks over our mouths and noses. It then feels like humanity is in limbo. This is inducing a considerable degree of fear, worry and concern in the population at large. Levels of anxiety, loneliness, depression, sleep and eating disorders, harmful alcohol and drug use, hyper or hypo sexuality, self-harm or suicidal and homicidal behaviour. Domestic and intimate partner violence are also on the rise.

Another major concern for the mental health workers are people with developing or pre-existing mental health conditions along with the mental health and well-being of frontline workers. A recent study conducted among 1200 health care workers from 34 hospitals in China providing COVID-19 care from January 29 to February 3, 2020, reported that health care workers presented with high levels of depression, anxiety, insomnia, and psychological distress (Lai J, Ma S, Wang Y, et al. 2019). Given the foregoing, it becomes critical for each individual to be aware and think of the best way to maintain their mental wellbeing during this crisis.

Mental health

In his effort to emphasis the importance of mental health, the first director general of WHO Dr. Brock Chisholm (1954) asserted that "there is no health without mental health". No wonder the WHO definition of health remains as "Health is a state of complete physical, mental and social well-being and not merely the absence of disease or infirmity" (WHO, 1948). Therefore, as the world continues to grapple with the physical effects of the Covid 19 pandemic, it becomes inevitable for the mental health practitioners to make people aware of the fact that the crisis has major effects on their inner beings. Yes, the physical effects from the covid-19 pandemic may be dealt with by use of physical medicine strategies by the end of the day. However, people's mental wellbeing whose effect may not be detected by infrared thermoguns or viral testing kits, if not dealt with might explode to an emotional and mental global pandemic in future.

According to the World Health Organization (WHO, 2004), mental health is "a state of well-being in which the individual realizes his or her own potential, can cope with the normal stresses of life, can work productively and fruitfully, and is able to make a contribution to his or her community." From this definition, mental wellbeing is at stake given the measures that have been put in place to control and combat the Covid-19 pandemic. Individuals feel that they are no longer in control of their abilities. Someone outside of us is dictating how we exploit our potentials. Even students in school have no control over how they perform. Workers cannot innovate or creatively do what they know how to do best. There is a lockdown which is not just physical but also mental. This has created a feeling of helplessness and hopelessness that deny some individuals the capacity to cope with normal daily stresses of life. After all, we are in a new normal. The question then remains what does "normal stresses of life" refer to in the new normal? Some are still asking "how do I remain productive and fruitful" when my job is gone, my business or career are not functional, or my learning institution has been closed down? The sense of autonomy or rather the ability to identify, confront, and solve problems seems dissipated.   The biblical maxim "the spirit indeed is willing, but the flesh is weak" has been reversed.

Many within the population claim that the body is willing but there is a lockdown which makes the spirit depressive. Contribution to one's community has become paradoxical with the containments, curfews, quarantines, social and physical distancing. Even those in the generativity stage of life are forced to mind their own business. If Erik Erickson lived in the Covid-19 days, he would probably have reviewed his stage-theory of psychosocial development. Thus, the need to remember that whatever has a beginning always has an end, hence the focus on mental well-being during and after the Covid-19 pandemic.

Mental well-being integrates mental health (mind), physical health (body) and Spiritual (Soul) resulting in more holistic approaches to disease prevention and mental health promotion. This means that the fight against the corona virus should also have a mental health trajectory since the mental health effects of this crisis can affect anyone regardless of age, gender, geographical location, social economic status, race/ethnicity, religion/ spirituality, sexual orientation, background or other aspect of cultural identity. The consequences of not addressing mental health conditions in this season may extend many years to come impairing both physical and mental health and limiting opportunities to lead fulfilling lives among many in the society.

Signs of losing the journey within

A common scientific fact points to the fact that no living organism wants to die neither the species to get extinct. That is why all living things react to threatening situations. Human beings are not exempt. The brain reacts by engaging the fight-flight gear in attempt to protect one from the looming danger. All the executive functions of the brain are put on hold; hence the reaction and feelings manifested. The thought of a disease that has no known cure can be overwhelming and cause strong emotions in both adults and children. Certain feelings and reactions are common in response to a highly emotionally significant situation like the Covid-19 pandemic, serious illness, loss of income, occupation and job or death of a loved one. This is normal when in a crisis. However, it is important to pay attention to reactions and behaviors that may be indicators that a person is not coping well. Some mental manifestations correspond to an understandable, transient response to the threatening experience. They can also be red flags of progression to a pathological condition which may be marked by change in personality, cognition and behavior.

Uncharacteristic emotions and behaviors that may be noted in self or others may include but not limited to;

- Reduced or Lack of sleep (insomnia) and changed sleep patterns. Sometimes preferring to engage in activities at night rather than going to bed. If depression is setting in, the person may oversleep.

- Unexplained anxiety and fears. A person may get panic attacks that makes them feel like there is no enough air in the room or say that they feel like they are about to die. Sometimes the physiological activities may manifest in terms of sweating, shaking, heart racing and fast shallow breaths.

- Poor eating habits for a person who was careful about diet should not be ignored. A person may show signs of poor appetite, overeating or use of wrong diet such as junk food and refined sugars. This could manifest in form of increased or decreased body weight.

- Physical symptoms that may be imagined or real manifest as body aches, coughs, diarrhea and so on which is referred to as somatization.

- A sense of hopelessness, feeling overwhelmed, helplessness and sometimes a talk of harm to self or to others. This could sometimes manifest as a "don't-care" attitude toward the protective measures that have been outlined by WHO, CDC, the Ministry of health and other stakeholders in the Covid-19 response. The person may neglect sanitizing the hands, wearing masks yet they are aware of the dangers of exposure. If the person had a pre-existing medical condition that requires regular medication, adherence to medication may become an issue.

- Tearfulness and feeling of sadness. Life seems meaningless and the mood becomes depressive most of the day.

- Anger and aggression or irritability. This could be in form of shouting to children and other people or fighting. This has increased the prevalence of domestic and intimate partner violence as well as child abuse in families. This is a displacement and projection of anger and frustration being experienced within. For parents, the feeling of being overstretched by the children's demand may manifest as aggression or abuse to children.

- If one is a people-person (extroverted), social isolation or withdrawal is an indicator that something is not well during this season. Teenagers and young adults may lock themselves up in their rooms or become rude to other family members as a signal to being left alone.

- For the children who are still learning at home, the level of concentration may be noted to be declining and sometimes it may appear like absent mindedness or day dreaming. In adolescents and adults this may present as loss of memory.

- Younger children who were independent may show regressive signs in form of becoming clingy, crying, wetting themselves, or wetting bed. Some may even start sucking their thumbs and talking like babies. Some may start experiencing night mares.

- Lack of self-care and personal neglect that could be in form of poor grooming, lack of taking a shower, or neglect to personal hygiene.

- Risky behaviors like use of drugs and alcohol either to keep calm (self-medication) or as a new habit due to idleness during the lockdown. Some may become hypersexual or hypo sexual especially that would be noted by spouses or partners. This has also increased cases of child sexual abuse or partner conflict during the Covid-19 crisis.

- Some people may start having hallucinations and delusions which may be confused for spirituality.

The above and any other signs that may manifest as a change of cognitions, emotions and behavior could serve as indicators that the Covid-19 crisis is or has taken a toll on a person even if they present like they are all together physically.

Steps that help to keep going: Coping Strategies

During a crisis like the Covid-19 pandemic, a person's coping mechanisms turn out to be insufficient; this is followed by a psychological imbalance and failure to adapt. It is important to note that every individual responds differently dependent on variables such as their genetic makeup, personality, health, earlier life experiences, social cultural environment, gender, age and so forth. Finding ways to cope with the Covid-19 stress will make you, the people you care about, and your community stronger. It is important to remember that there is a way out if we focus on life after the pandemic. Healthy coping mechanisms will bring about calmness and reduce anxiety. The following recommendations may help navigate and handle the Covid-19 crisis with the dynamics it has brought to our lives.

Validate the feelings: Accept to self that it is normal to

worry and feel threatened by what is happening. As the cabinet Secretary MOH in Kenya keeps asserting, "this thing is real and its treating us abnormally" (Kagwe, 2020) referring to the corona virus. Acknowledging that it is understandable to feel anxious and worried about what may happen, especially when many aspects of life are uncertain or have changed is okay. Healing begins with acknowledgment that one is sick or has an issue that needs to be dealt with or managed. It also helps to name the specific feelings that are being experienced without feeling ashamed. This could be shared with family or significant others.

Information is power: There are several conspiracy theories surrounding the Covid-19 situation. It is, therefore, imperative to get the correct information surrounding this pandemic. Seek information only from trusted sources such as the WHO, CDC or MOH websites so that you can take practical and correct measures to mitigate against this pandemic. You could also call or talk with medics and scientists who understand the corona virus, its health implications and protective measures. Some sources of information like social media may give false information that may exacerbate mental health issues or that may endanger you and other people. For example recently a social media message was advocating the use of alcohol as a protective measure against the corona virus. It was later discovered that the source of the short message did not understand the difference between alcohol-based sanitizer and drinking alcohol. Authentic information calms one and as the bible says; "the truth sets one free". Facts help balance between instilling fear and taking the correct protective measures.

Minimal exposure to Covid-19 media reports: The sudden and near-constant stream of news reports about an outbreak can cause anyone to feel worried. Watching, reading or listening to news about Covid-19 that causes an individual to feel anxious or distressed is not good for mental well-being. There seems to be information overload with constant news about Covid-19 from all types of media which can heighten fears about the disease. Limit social media that may expose one to rumors and false information too. Also limit reading, hearing or watching other news if it causes you emotional imbalance, but keep up to date on global, national, and local recommendations. You could ask a significant other to update you on the days you feel overwhelmed. This helps to set limits on worry time by refocusing on other pleasurable activities such as baking, knitting, playing board games, cooking other activities that could cover that news hour or time spent on social media.

Daily routine. Try as much as possible to keep your personal daily routines or create new routines if circumstances change like if put in quarantine. Maintaining a regular schedule is important to one's mental health. In addition, sticking to a regular bedtime routine, keeping consistent times for meals, bathing and getting dressed up, work or study schedules and exercise helps the mind to feel organized and motivated to accomplish something in a day. This predictability can also make one feel more in control. It is also good to set aside time for activities one enjoys which help garner positive energy to move on. For those working at home, keep a to-do list and follow your diary. It helps to feel like life is still moving on normally. There is need to also plan some "me" time. This helps one to get in touch with self especially since families are locked down in the same space.

Social Support Systems: Human beings are social creatures. Social connectedness has been curtailed by the crisis situation we are in. This cuts off the social support which is key to recovery from both physical and mental illness. There is need to repackage ourselves and still keep the connection since we don't know how long this pandemic will take. Families and friends should keep connected via digital platforms. They can hold virtual gatherings and enjoy the presence of one another while still keeping the physical distance. For the religious groups, people can still hold their services, fellowships and bible studies virtually. Groups and families can still pray, worship and dance together. For those without complicated electronic devices or without internet connection, teleconferencing, short messages and personal calls work to keep one connected with the social support system. It's important to note that social problems may emerge such as breakdown of community support systems and stigma against the vulnerable and ill. If a family member or friend needs to be quarantined for safety reasons or gets sick and needs to be in isolation at home or in the hospital, come up with ways to stay in contact. This could be through electronic devices or the telephone or by sending a note to brighten the day. People are also coming up with creative ways of offering social support. Recently, a gentleman I was supporting in quarantine, had his friends drive to the road outside near the hotel he was in and through the window of his room, they would wave and communicate love to him nonverbally. This he said helped him feel loved and connected during his 21 days. For employers, be empathetic and affirm your employees who may not be coping. Families are encouraged to keep together and have family debriefs where every member is allowed to share how the pandemic is impacting them. Every person has his or her own way of expressing emotions. The other members would then accord the necessary support.

Positive thoughts and restructured cognitions: Choose to focus and amplify the positive things in life, instead of dwelling on how bad one feels or how dire the situation looks. Consider starting each day by listing things you are thankful for. Maintain a sense of hope, work to accept changes as they occur and try to keep problems in perspective. For example, if put in quarantine, think of the good that could comes from the fourteen or so days of isolation. If a source of livelihood has been lost think of how to access basic needs without having to worry about major things. If overwhelmed by the fear of contracting the illness, read or listen to stories of people who have recovered from Covid-19 or who have supported a loved one and are willing to share their experience. Bank on past experiences when you went through a crisis and you overcame. It gives hope to the person that it is still possible to overcome the current crisis.

Establish personal choices that give healthy coping: During a crisis, it's advisable to engage in healthy activities that one enjoys and finds relaxing. Exercise regularly. This could be done in the house or room. Keep regular sleep routines and eat healthy food. This could be accomplished by maintaining good sleep hygiene and by avoiding use of stimulants like coffee or watching negative stimulating movies at least two hours before sleeping time. Get to bed and sleep and do not use a phone while in bed. In case you have problem falling asleep, avoid taking sleeping pills or reaching for a glass of alcoholic drinks. Be careful to abide by the government directives and not to be caught off guard by the government for instance being caught out during curfew hours. For those in town or crowded houses, find ways of going to an open place to have a shout or stretch. It psychologically relieves the lockdown effect.

Connecting with God: Spirituality is a protective factor against mental distress. Seek the person and the presence of God through prayer and other regular spiritual exercises such as reading and meditating on the scriptures, emphasize communion with God, thinking His thoughts, sensing His presence, and knowing His will. This changes the focus from self to a higher power that is able to give a solution to the crisis.

Establish referral pathways for help: There are several players in the Covid-19 response. It is important to have access and knowledge to the available avenues for help. This may include the chief, police service, ambulances, health services, spiritual leaders and psychosocial support services. There are helpline contacts attached to all these responders that may assist in case you are stuck.

Conclusion

From the above conversation, it is obvious that our lives have been changed by the emergence of the Covid-19 pandemic that has led to significant change in what we knew as normal life. This poses many new challenges that require several coping mechanisms. Some people are at greater risk of poor mental health. This chapter has opened a candid conversation on how the Covid-19 crisis could be maneuvered without one breaking from within. We can expect the current strong feelings to fade when the pandemic is over, but stress won't disappear from life when the health crisis of Covid-19 ends. There is need to continue with these practices to take care of mental health and increase the ability to cope with life's ongoing challenges.

REFERENCES

Lai J , Ma S , Wang Y , et al., (2020)., Factors associated with mental health outcomes among health care workers exposed to coronavirus disease 2019.   JAMA Netw Open. 2020;3(3):e203976.doi:10.1001/jamanetworkopen.2020.3976 ArticlePubMedGoogle Scholar

World Health Organization (2004). Promoting mental health: concepts, emerging evidence, practice (Summary Report) Geneva: World Health Organization.

Opportunity in Crisis

By Rev. Paul Njoroge, Senior Pastor, CITAM Clay City

The word crisis when written in Chinese has two parts into it. The first part is about danger and the second part is about opportunity.

John F Kennedy

The default setting during crisis is to concentrate on the danger at hand and how to deal with it.This unfortunately makes people miss opportunities that the crisis presents. This is informed by the way we are wired as human beings—that crisis is something that must be done away with as quickly as possible. The body detests pain and hence it also works in getting rid of any situation that causes discomfort.

Though not celebrated, crisis often provides a great opportunity that if well explored can change a person, family, organization, country trajectory for the better. Some of the biggest corporations in the world that have been in existence for many years do so because they keep reinventing themselves even when threatened by predicaments. The gospel expansion too rides on waves of crisis. During the reign of Emperor Nero, a fierce persecutor of followers of Christ, the disciples were scattered abroad and spread the gospel everywhere they went. Acts 8:1-4 records, "On that day a great persecution broke out against the church in Jerusalem, and all except the apostles were scattered throughout

Judea and Samaria. Godly men buried Stephen and mourned deeply for him. But Saul began to destroy the church. Going from house to house, he dragged off both men and women and put them in prison. Those who had been scattered preached the word wherever they went." Apostle Paul writing to the Romans said that all things work together for the good of those who love the lord. All things mean both good and bad. It is therefore imperative to glean for the good in every situation.

COVID-19 is a crisis that everybody in the world is facing. Everyone including the rich and the poor, black and white, young and old, are feeling the pinch of this pandemic. The economy too has not been spared. Many countries of the world are staring at unprecedented possible recession. In such circumstances, the human tendency is to think about saving one's life. 'Everybody for his own, God for us all', people would say. With the economic downturn affecting everybody and social distancing becoming the new normal, the opportunities this crisis brings may not be as obvious. The truth, however is, this pandemic provides many opportunities to change many things for the better. One can also ask, what would Jesus do in such a situation and what would He want us to do?

Replacing Bad News with the Good News

As I alluded earlier, throughout history, the gospel expansion accelerates through times of crisis. This, therefore, means that time is ripe for sharing of the Good news in the midst of the hopeless situation the masses are experiencing. In this Covid-19 crisis, information available on social media, radio and TV is basically tends to be bad news – the number of infections, deaths, economic problems, etc. This news can be very discouraging, to say the least. As a matter of fact, psychologists are projecting a rise in cases of depression and stress related issues. A reduction of time spent on these news and information forums is important for mental health.

On the other hand, despite the reality of bad news, scripture provides the greatest comfort by pointing people to God. Isaiah 26:3 says, "he keeps in perfect peace whose mind is stayed on him". As someone observed, we can never avoid strife in the world around us, but when we fix our thoughts on God, we can know perfect peace, even in turmoil. As we focus our minds on God and his word, we become steady and stable (NLT bible notes on Isaiah 26:3). It is, therefore, prudent that we become carriers of the good news that all is not lost, and that God is in charge.

Matthew 11:28 says, "Come to me, all you who are weary and burdened, and I will give you rest." This is a great reminder that we have a place we can cast our cares to, and that is on Christ. One does not need to struggle through life issues alone and especially so with the Covid-19 related challenges. You can allow Jesus Christ to become the close friend who is able to change your frowning into a smiles, and the gripe into a song.

A Great Opportunity of Sharing with the Needy.

The bible says that every time Jesus met a crowd, he was moved by compassion. This was not only because of spiritual needs but also because of the physical needs he saw. The bible records two incidences where he fed multitudes of 4000 and 5000. In Matthew 25, a guideline on what he will use to determine who enters the joy of the father are those who visited him in jail, gave him food, and clothed him. Jesus pointed out that the good that was done to the needy was as though it was unto him.

Even though everybody is affected economically by the pandemic, there are those among us who are hit harder. 65% of the Kenyan population are those who are in business or what are commonly known as jua kali sector. These are people who depend on daily income for their daily provisions. With the partial lockdown, it means that there is no business at all, or they have already closed altogether. Sharing does not only happen because we have more than enough, but we are called to share the little we have. Luke 3:11 "Anyone who has two shirts should share with the one who has none, and anyone who has food should do the same." Humanity is tested on how we care for fellow man. Apostle Paul writing to Galatians says to them that it is when we bear each other's burden that we fulfill the law of Christ (Gal 6:2).

This should not just be at the individual level, but also corporate bodies should also join in providing relief to the affected persons. CITAM (Christ is the Answer Ministries) for instance, started an initiative dubbed the Bread of Life. This creates an opportunity for members of the congregation to pool together funds to reach out to the most vulnerable in the society by providing electronic food vouchers.

A Great Opportunity to Pray

"God whispers to us in our pleasures, speaks in our conscience, but shouts in our pains: it is his megaphone to rouse a deaf world." (C.S. Lewis).

It's quite encouraging to see the many prayers being offered in the world today because of corona virus. Nations are calling for national day of prayer. As believers we have an amazing opportunity to pray for the nations to turn to God. 2 Chronicles 7:14 "if my people, who are called by my name, will humble themselves and pray and seek my face and turn from their wicked ways, then will I hear from heaven and will forgive their sin and will heal their land." It appears that God is calling the nations of the world to repent, and hence believers can use this opportunity to pray earnestly for the deliverance of the world. The reality is that many Christians have been slowed down by lockdowns hence more time in their hands to pray. Plus, people have been pushed to desperation to the extent that they are compelled to reach out to supreme power of God.

COVID-19 has exposed the limitations of science, and believers should continue seeking the face of the Lord because prayer is our response when foundations are shaken. There are great testimonies already of answered prayer. A testimony from Dr. Julian Urban, a 38-year-old serving in a hospital in Lombardy, Italy, attests:

Never in my darkest nightmares did I imagine that I would see and experience what has been going on in Italy in our hospital the past three weeks. The nightmare flows, and the river gets bigger and bigger. At first, a few patients came, then dozens, and then hundreds. Now, we are no longer doctors, but sorters who decide who should live and who should be sent home to die, though all these patients paid Italian health taxes throughout their lives." Until two weeks ago, my colleagues and I were atheists. It was normal because we are doctors. We learned that science excludes the presence of God. I laughed at my parents going to church. Nine days ago, a 75-year-old pastor was admitted into the hospital. He was a kind man. He had serious breathing problems. He had a Bible with him and impressed us by how he read it to the dying as he held their hand. We the doctors were all tired, discouraged, psychologically and physically finished. When we had time, we listened to him. We have reached our limits. We can do no more. People are dying every day. We are exhausted. We have two colleagues who have died, and others that have been infected. We realized that we needed to start asking God for help. We do this when we have a few free minutes. When we talk to each other, we cannot believe that, though we were once fierce atheists, we are now daily in search of peace, asking the Lord to help us continue so that we can take care of the sick. (Julian Urban, 2020)

A Great Opportunity to Build Family Relationships

For a long time because of the busyness of life especially in many urban centers, families are rarely together. However, due to measures issued by governments including lockdown - whether full or partial, family members are now back home together. These restrictions provide an opportunity for families to reestablish their good foundations. This calls for willingness and being deliberate, despite the challenges involved. Children learn best by observing, therefore, the parents can take advantage of this time that circumstances have brought them together, to model to their children, best life practices and values.

However, the National Council on Administration of Justice (NACJ) has reported "a significant spike in Gender Based Violence in many parts of the country during this season." This is a grim reality that we need to be aware of. Suffering in silence can have serious consequences. One can seek help from the authorities, and their spiritual leaders.

Opportunity to Review Priorities

It has been said that life for many people is like a rat race, chasing that piece of cheese and the moment you get it you discover that you want more. In the face of Covid-19, all the things we thought matter are basically useless. Wealth and life pleasures have been exposed for what their true nature is, vanity. The funny thing about COVID-19, is that the effects do not segregate, for both poor and rich are affected.

We are slowly learning that life is not a sub total of material things, but it is the simple things of life that make it interesting - family, food to eat and a roof over one's head. What this crisis is teaching the world is the discipline of simplicity. What you have or where you derive your joy from may be taken away any time.

We are at a place as a nation where the sins of corruption have caught up with us. The health care systems are so weak. The government and her people can only hope that the pandemic slows down. All these years, many governments have concentrated on military advancements, infrastructure developments and heavy industrialization with inadequate attention given to health care. Yet now we are all reminded what is really important. With this reality, it is prudent for individuals and nations to reset priorities. To pursue justice and honour with what we do and how we manage what has been entrusted to us.

Servant Leadership in Stormy Seasons

By Pete Ondeng, Founder, Lead Africa Foundation

One of the most famous expressions on leadership is a statement drawn from Alice in Wonderland, the 1865 novel written by English author, Lewis Carroll. In the story, the main character, Alice, is engaged in a conversation with the Cheshire Cat. Alice informs the cat that she wants to go somewhere and needs direction. The cat asks Alice where she would like to go, but she does not know where. She just wants to go somewhere. The Cheshire Cat responds and says, "If you don't know where you are going, then it doesn't really matter which way you go; any road will take you there."

The COVID-19 pandemic has blown a wind of confusion in society, throwing many people, organizations and nations off their beaten tracks. Maps and landmarks that guided their footsteps and gave meaning to their journeys seem no longer relevant. Priorities, goals, traditions and even values that defined their existence have been brought into question. With the thick dust of death and destruction still swirling in the air, we can hear the question on everybody's mind: Where do we go from here?

There is no simple answer to the question, but it is a question that must be answered. We all know that we cannot turn the clock back and return to where we were, but we also know that we cannot stay where we are. We must go somewhere.

How does a leader lead in a time of such uncertainty? How do you lead when you are as vulnerable as the sheep you lead, and your eyes are stinging from the same smoke that is blinding your followers?

A pastor who led a flock and built a church through hard toil, grit and diligence, suddenly finds himself without a pulpit, without income and without the symbolic trappings of leadership. An entrepreneur who commanded respect and found pride in being able to provide employment to others stands dazed in the marketplace with little more than debts to show for all his work. A politician who built a following and found relevance in front of the crowds, sits at home, staring at the television for something – anything that might point to somewhere.

Where do we go from here? The question hangs in the air like a suspended object. Everyone has an opinion. The Cheshire Cat in Alice in Wonderland found an answer to the question that Alice put to him. His answer was a question that men and women in leadership should embrace as backbone of their leadership playbook during this time of uncertainty: Where would you like to go? The question shifts the spotlight from the desires and objectives of the leader and directs it back to those that he or she leads. It is their needs, their fears, their aspirations and their successes that must be the leader's preoccupation. It is in that pursuit of the interests of others that true, godly leadership is shaped.

The playbook on leadership that guided many leaders in the old world seemed to accentuate attributes like courage, boldness, focus and self-discipline. These attributes are generally aligned with traditional, top-down leadership models. These models generally subscribe to a definition of leadership that expects leaders to influence their followers to pursue a common interest or achieve a common, pre-determined goal. This typically positions leaders as being in-charge and/or in-control and reinforces the traditional leader-follower construct.

An alternative set of leadership attributes what would seem so much more applicable to stormy seasons like that brought about by the COVID pandemic would be compassion, selflessness, sacrifice and patience. These attributes do not point so much to what a leader does as much as to what a leader is. They speak of servant leadership, a concept that has been written about and discussed for years, but which is never more relevant than in times of great tribulation. Servant leadership is not about leaders who serve, but rather, servants who lead. They lead, not by command or manipulation, but by building trust and influence from their dedication to helping other people succeed.

In the context of the COVID-19 pandemic, the world has been thrown into an unprecedented, multi-dimensional crisis that is not only physical, but also psychological and spiritual. The need for authentic, caring leaders to hold society together, restore hope and dignity at this time of uncertainty cannot be over emphasized. The environment for leadership is not only shaky, but it is also may have little reward in the near term.

The drastic responses by world governments to the pandemic have caused pain and gripped the world with a collective fear of the unknown. People who have lost their livelihoods feel exposed and vulnerable. The travel restrictions, curfews and lockdown orders by governments may be necessary, but the human spirit yearns for freedom. The prospects of social unrest are high.

Because of hunger and joblessness, criminal activity is likely to increase. Due to reduced economic activity, governments will struggle to pay civil service salaries, resulting in compromised public services like healthcare and education. Allegations of corruption in the use of government resources could further aggravate an already volatile situation. Respect for authority diminishes and gives way to a spirit of rebellion.

In some countries, such as South Africa and Nigeria, the military has been called out of the barracks to ensure compliance with government directives. The battle lines between a nation and the Corona virus slowly morphs into a battle between the government and its own people. These are the stark realities and the potential backdrop against which a new breed of servant leaders must emerge.

Anyone aspiring to be an effective leader in these turbulent times should adopt a posture of listening – first to God who, through the life of Jesus on earth, provided a perfect template. In Mathew 20:28, Jesus famously says, "Just as the Son of Man did not come to be served, but to serve, and to give his life as a ransom for many."

A servant leader is a shepherd. A shepherd exists for one thing, and one thing only: to take care of the sheep. This is the secret to greatness. Amazingly, it is also the most difficult and most elusive lesson of all in the realm of leadership.

A true servant leader wanting to be relevant in this historical moment must recognize his limitations. No man or woman can, on their own, bear the burden of troubled, fearful and agitated people without supernatural help. In this regard, listening to God is more than a casual exercise.

The world needs leaders who will go to the mountain and listen to God. Hearing directly from God will give the leader the grace, the conviction and the peace to keep serving even through, darkness, persecution, and personal need.

Reimagining a Post-COVID-19 Future: Lessons from Church History

By Rev. Lucas Owako,...

When faced with new, yet monumental, challenges such as the COVID-19 pandemic, communities look into their existing resources in search of explanations for the present and prescriptions for the future. One such arsenal for the global Christian community is the study of its history. Mark Noll says the following about studying the history of Christianity:

> Study of the past can be useful in shaping proper Christian attitudes. It is often easier in reviewing the past than in looking at the present to discriminate between matters that are absolutely essential to genuine Christianity and those that are either of relative importance or not important at all. If we are able to isolate from past generations what was of crucial significance in the church's mission, then we have a chance in the present to order our emotional and spiritual energies with discrimination – preserving our deepest commitment only for those aspects of Christian faith that deserve such commitment and acting with ever greater toleration as we move from the centre of the faith to its periphery (Noll, 2012).

In seeking to draw from the rich resources of the history of Christianity towards informing the response to the current pandemic, this paper explores how four historical moments of global upheaval affected and shaped the church, and then draws some lessons from these for the present.

Examples of Moments of Volatility in Church History

The Antonine Plague (167-180 CE) and the Plague of Cyprian (250-270 CE)

These two pestilences, later thought to have been the initial outbreaks of smallpox and measles respectively, swept through the Roman Empire with devastating consequences. They killed significant proportions of the population including Emperors, depleted armies, destroyed the economy, and generally soaked the empire in suffering and misery. While Rome experienced an almost all round decline, there was some kind of religious renaissance, touching on pagan Greco-Roman religions as well as nascent Christianity. Sarah Yeomans explains this phenomenon with the observation that "Human beings, both ancient and modern, tend to be more open to considerations of the divine in times of fear and in the face of imminent mortality... It seems that the ancient Romans, in the face of an inexplicable and incurable epidemic, turned to the divine" (Yeomans, 2017).

Rodney Stark suggests three reasons why these epidemics had significant contribution to the explosive growth of Christianity. First, the epidemics proved to be beyond the explanatory and comforting capacities of existing religions and philosophies. Christianity was able to offer a more viable explanation for the epidemics, and with it a more positive outlook for the future. Secondly, the Christian virtue of selfless love was translated by believers into community solidarity and social service. This resulted into greater survival rates among Christians and made their faith more appealing to their neighbours. Thirdly, when the epidemics shattered existing social bonds and cleavages, the Christian community, bound together by faith and virtue as seen above, remained as a viable and appealing alternative (Stark, 1997).

The Bubonic Plague of 1527

The bubonic plague, also known as "the black death", swept through Germany in 1527. When it reached Wittenberg, the university leadership decided to move the university to Jena and urged Luther, together with other professors, to move for their safety. Luther, however, declined and stayed in Wittenberg through the plague. In response to a query from Johann Hess who was in Breslau in Silesia, Luther wrote an advisory to the clergy on whether it was proper for a Christian to flee from such a deadly peril. This advisory highlights two key points:

First, in a conviction that touches on one of the key questions for the church around COVID-19, Luther classified the pastor among the essential services that must stay to take care of the sick and dying. The pastor, he said, being a shepherd and not a hireling, is commanded by Christ to risk possible death because he is needed by the flock for comfort and strength in the hour of death. "In time of death one is especially in need of the ministry which can strengthen and comfort one's conscience with God's Word and Sacrament in order to overcome death with faith." He proceeded to advise that in cases where there are already enough ministers to perform these critical duties, then others were at liberty to move away and stay safe. Fleeing from death, he argued, is not sinful in itself and so long as the needs of those to whom one has charge are met, there is wisdom in moving away. Luther applied the same guidance to "all other persons who are bound to others by duties and responsibilities."

Secondly, was an advisory against an ever-present temptation of overzealous Christians to presume too much on God's protection as to sinfully become "too daring and foolhardy," tempting God and overlooking the need for protective and medical care. Of such, Luther said:

> That would not be well done. Use medicine. Take whatever may be helpful to you. Fumigate your house, yard, and street. Avoid persons and places where you are not needed or where your neighbour has recovered. Act as one who would like to help put out a general fire... Meanwhile think thus: "With God's permission the enemy has sent poison and deadly dung among us, and so I will pray to God that he may be gracious and preserve us. Then I will fumigate to purify the air, give and take medicine, and avoid places and persons where I am not needed in order that I may not abuse myself and that through me others may not be infected and inflamed with the result that I become the cause of their death through my negligence. If God wishes to take me, he will be able to find me. At least I have done what he gave me to do and am responsible neither for my own death nor for the death of others. But if my neighbour needs me, I shall avoid neither person nor place but feel free to visit and help him," as has already been said. Behold, this is a true and God-fearing faith which is neither foolhardy nor rash and does not tempt God (Luther, 1955).

The Great Depression of the 1930s

This severe economic depression started in the United States of America and swept through the rest of the world in the 1930s. While most major evangelical denominations had challenges significantly addressing the need of the moment in a fresh, proactive and creative way, the newer and smaller, mostly Pentecostal denominations sought to engage with the need of the hour. Their theologians had a threefold explanation of the great depression: First, was an eschatological vision that saw it as a prelude to the Second Coming. Secondly was to view the socioeconomic misfortunes as blessings from God, sent to prompt people towards repentance, revival and reform. Thirdly, they saw it as an invitation to shift focus from trusting in other things to trusting in God and proving his faithfulness. The result was a broader outlook, interpreting their struggles in light of the suffering their brothers and sisters around the world were undergoing, and resulting into greater missionary fervour. By the end of the period, these previously smaller denominations had gained greater membership and global visibility (Curtis, 2011).

The 2nd World War

The 2nd World War was another time of global upheaval with significant implications for Christianity. Although the immediate post-war period saw renewed religious fervour as people trooped to churches, this trend was soon upstaged by the secularism, liberalism and globalization that emerged from the same events (Beckman, 2000). These trends climaxed in the 1960s and 1970s, forcing American evangelicalism into retreat mode, especially in its public proclamation. Mark Shaw says the following concerning Billy Graham, by far the most visible face of America's post-war evangelicalism:

Graham came under new attack not just from his fundamentalist critics but from the cultural elite. Winning people to Christ through personal evangelism seemed in bad taste. With the strange new world of sexual freedom, civil rights and radical politics sweeping youth culture in the sixties, Graham struggled to remain relevant. In a way that had not been true before, he took up Torrey Johnson's second goal: The evangelisation of the world. In that new pursuit, he found a new ally [in Pentecostalism] (Shaw, 2010).

Volatility and the Opportunity for Revitalization

The Evangelical Renewal Movement (ERM) theory posits that moments of volatility have often been cradles of significant renewal. One of its leading proponents, Anthony Wallace, says that "Revitalization is, from a cultural standpoint, a special kind of culture change phenomenon: the persons involved in the process of revitalization must perceive their culture, or some major areas of it, as a system...; they must feel that this cultural system is unsatisfactory; and they must innovate not merely discrete items, but a new cultural system, specifying new relationships as well as, in some cases; new traits." In this case, then, revitalisation necessarily springs from situations of volatility and brokenness. Wallace proceeds to identify a three-stage pattern of revitalization that involves, first, the problem stage in which people conclude that their frameworks for interpreting and responding to realities no longer suffice. Secondly, is the paradigm stage in which new leadership emerges from the brokenness of the previous stage, offering new interpretations of reality as well as relationships and frameworks for response. The third, is the power stage in which a new movement emerges, faces and overcomes resistance from the old order, and a new norm is established, under new leadership (Wallace, 2003).

It is now a widely recognised reality that COVID-19 has disrupted global systems so significantly that, in ways yet to be experienced, what has hitherto been "normal" is dead, and the world awaits the unveiling of a new but different normal. The global economy is so shaken that nobody knows for sure how long it will take for it to stabilize again. Globalization with its interconnectedness and interdependency has been shaken. Nations are realizing that openness can bring untold suffering, and that interdependency can lead to crippling vulnerability. With human interactions presenting mortal danger, people have retreated to the digital space in ways previously difficult to imagine. On the religious front, people are having to figure out how to worship, and do mission in new ways. This disruption is reshaping values, perspectives and worldviews.

This context, then, provides a great opportunity for revitalization. Looking at church history presents several lessons on how the church can navigate through the present as it shapes the future.

Applying the Lessons to COVID-19 Response

Discerning and letting go of what is dying

Not all explanations and prescriptions that the church has hitherto had will suffice for the present moment. This calls for quick discernment so as to know what to let go. In the pre-Christian and Roman society, Christianity became a fresh alternative to the unsatisfactory philosophies and pagan religions that preceded it. In contrast, the post-war Western society did not hesitate to seek new explanations and prescriptions away from the prevalent Christendom, and quickly shifted towards what has now been called a post-Christian society. How is Africa likely to respond to the COVID-19 upheaval?

Listening to the society, especially the liberalized social media, one would not fail to notice an emboldened and louder questioning, criticism and even mockery of Christianity. The African Christian will most likely have to contend with what the Psalmist before her, as well as her Western counterpart, contended with: "My tears have been my food day and night, while people say to me all day long, "Where is your God?" (Psalm 42:3)

She is shocked that, unlike in the time of Luther and the bubonic plague, the state does not consider church one of the essential services. The health and wealth teaching that has been so prevalent in the Continent is receiving renewed focus, as people ask in jest: "wouldn't this be a good time to demonstrate your miraculous powers of healing and wealth creation?"[4] Furthermore, the churches that have been full for decades are now empty, with people learning to do church at home, and there is no telling how many of them will troop back when calm is finally restored. Finally, there is no telling the extent to which these changes will affect the Christians' ability to witness and speak for Christ in the public space.

The church's ability to effectively re-imagine the future, therefore, begins with an accurate discernment of the present and identification of the aspects of her theology

---

[4] An interesting development, probably mirrored elsewhere, has emerged in South Africa where the government has announced a 26 billion US dollars' stimulus package accompanying a 35-day lockdown. Church leaders are shocked that the stimulus package has thought of almost everyone else but them, even though everyone knows churches are locked and church workers have no means of income at the moment.

and practice that have been shaken. How does she deal with reduced public confidence and sympathy? How does she balance the biblical view of the metaphysical with the need for rational explanations of reality? How does she deal with a declining voice in public affairs? How does she continue to do mission amongst a disapproving and in some cases suspicious or hostile populace? How does she deal with declining membership and income? Furthermore, in the likely event that eradication of the virus becomes impossible or a long drawn out affair, how will the mega churches, especially in the cities, manage years in which "social distancing" becomes a basic necessity?

COVID-19, therefore, demands that the church puts all that is not indispensable essential doctrines on the table, and identify what is shaken or fading and needs to be dropped, and then employ enlightened imagination to establish alternatives from what is emerging.

Making the most of our "stick in the hand"

There is a Swahili saying that "fimbo ya mbali haiui nyoka" (a remote stick – that is far – cannot kill a snake). During moments of crisis like now, it is difficult to begin inventing. An example is presence in the digital space. Churches that were already engaging, even minimally, have had a significant head start, while those that had ignored the digital space have found it near impossible to start from zero. Similarly, it is critical to ask what the church has at hand, that will be useful in meeting the needs of the moment. From the plagues of the 2nd and 3rd centuries, to the bubonic plague of the 16th century, the Christian virtues of love and selfless service have been the most outstanding. The American church after the great depression and in the post-war era found new relevance in missional engagements. For some reason, as church history demonstrates, sacrificial love neither goes wrong not expires.

This, then, is a time for the church not to be inward looking, focusing on own challenges and struggles. When the dust settles on the pandemic, people will remember those who were with them when their loved ones were dying, alone and lonely, in isolation wards. They will remember the churches that facilitated video calls with those who were sick and dying, when physical visits were disallowed by the state. They will remember those churches that emptied their coffers to put food on the table for those who suddenly lost their income and, stuck in their houses, did not know where the next meal for their children would come from. They will remember those who donated phones for their children to be able to follow lessons online. They will remember those who called just to find out how they were doing.

Towards a new relevance

Church history teaches us that, even in times of volatility, God has always had a path into the future. He has sustained the church even when the church has really struggled to be faithful to her calling and mission (Noll, 2012). Unfortunately, there have also been moments when sections of the church have fallen into serious decline. While the universal church will never end as long as Christ tarries, history does show that sections of it have from time to time declined and even folded up. It thus follows that while believers let go of the past and reappraise their available tools for the future, they also need to be cognizant of the reality that sections of the church (local churches, denominations, regions) will experience significant decline and even death. The

ERM theory holds that, after the problem phase, if the paradigm phase does not bring fresh relationships and ideas, the power stage becomes unattainable, and the result is decline and death (Wallace, 2003).

The difference, in the present case, will be in the church's ability to provide a relevant ministry, founded on a relevant contextual theology and expressed in responsive action. As John Gatu says, Christian theology has to be practical for it to be meaningful and useful, otherwise it will fall victim to the caution in the African proverb: what original language is this proverb? Can we have it in the form too? "I have a cow in the sky, but I cannot drink her milk" (Gatu, 2006).

What, then, would be some of the questions that people will be asking in the immediate aftermath of COVID-19, that believers need to prayerfully find answers for today? These would include:

i.   Economic empowerment following global recession

ii.   The usefulness of congregational worship and pastoral care

iii.   The necessity of physical meetings instead of online "fellowship".

iv.   How to respond to the probing questions of the agnostic.

v.   New frontiers and methods for mission

vi.   How to mitigate and even ride on a potential rolling back on globalisation, especially with regards to global movements, trade and aid.

vii.   Etc.

As seen in the examples from church history outlined above, the answers to these questions will require relevant theologies, relevant actions, and new networks and partnerships. The time to work on these is now, while it is still day. The churches that will outlast and thrive after COVID-19 will most likely be those that are successful in this endeavor.

Conclusion

Church history, therefore, comforts us that the present challenge is not the first and worst. Our brethren have, at other times in other places, gone through the same and worse. It assures us that God has always been present with his people, and has availed kingdom resources that can help us navigate. It demonstrates to us that such providence can help us turn around this situation of death into a new, revitalized movement. But it also cautions that such renewal will not come from a posture of mediocrity, but rather from active and discerning engagement with the past, the present and the future.

REFERENCES

Beckman, J. (2000, October). Religion in Post-World War II America. Retrieved April 20, 2020 from National Humanities' Centre: http://nationalhumanitiescenter.org/tserve/twenty/tkeyinfo/trelww2.htm

Brown, J. (n.d.). From https://www.brainyquote.com/quotes/h_jackson_brown_jr_134502

Buechner, F. (2017, July 18). From https://www.frederickbuechner.com/quote-of-the-day/2017/7/18/vocation

Buford, B. (2008). Halftime: Moving from Success to Significance. Grand Rapids, Michigan: Zondervan.

Curtis, H. D. (2011). God is Not Affected by the Great

Depression. Pentecostal Missions During the 1930s , 80 (3), 579-589.

Ford, H. (n.d.). From http://www.ft.lk/columns/surround-yourself-with-the-best-people-you-can-find/4-69735

Gatu, J. (2006). Joyfully Christian and Joyfully African. Nairobi: Acton.

Goleman, D. (1996). Emotional Intelligence: Why it Can Matter More Than IQ. Bloomsbury.

Goleman, D. (2004, January). What Makes a Leader? Harvard Business Review , 1-10.

Leipzig, A. (2013, February 1). How to Know Your Life Purpose in 5 Minutes. From https://youtu.be/vVsXO9brK7M?list=PL5qZYippVH6nQWgF4jhUOZEAPRsx0df_A

Luther, M. (1955). Advice in Time of Epidemic and Famine. In M. Luther, & T. G. Tappert (Ed.), Letters of Spiritual Counsel (pp. 228-257). Westminster: Westminster Press.

Maxwell, J. C. (2003, January 3). Leadership 101.

Noll, M. A. (2012). Turning Points: Decisive Moments in the History of Christianity (3rd ed.). Grand Rapids, Michigan: Baker Academic.

Palmer, P. J. (2000). Let Your Life Speak: Listening for the Voice of Vocation. John Wiley & Sons, Inc.

Pearce, N. (2019). The Purpose Path: A Guide to Pursuing Your Authentic Work. New York: St Martin's Press.

Piper, J. (2020). Coronavirus and Christ. Wheaton, IL: Crossway.

Shaw, M. (2010). Global Awakening: How 20th Century Revivals Triggered a Christian Revolution. Downers Grove, Illinois: IVP Academic.

Stark, R. (1997). The Rise of Christianity: How the Obscure, Marginal Jesus Movement Became the Dominant Religious Force in the Western World in a Few Centuries. San-Francisco:

Harper.

Wallace, A. F. (2003). Revitalization Movements. In R. S. Grumet (Ed.), Revitalizations and Mazeways. Lincoln, Nebraska: University of Nebraska.

Warren, R. (1997). What am I Here For? The Purpose Driven Life. Zondervan.

Yeomans, S. (2017). The Antonine Plague and the Spread of Christianity. Biblical Archaeology Review , 43, 24-66.

People, Power, and the Pandemic

By Dr. Mary Thamari, Social Anthropologist and Development Practitioner

"I have seen the affliction of my PEOPLE. I have heard their cry of distress. Yes, I am aware of their suffering." (Exodus 3:7)

We would imagine that since the corona virus is infecting people, then it would be obvious that people would be at the centre of all our reflections and actions. At the time of writing this article, 41 days after declaration of the pandemic, corona word in google search generated 937 million words in 0.25 seconds. For a word that is strictly scientific and whose prominence rose in late 2019, that's enormous! Undoubtedly, the virus had gripped the hearts of kings, the minds of scientists and the breath of the infected, literally. We have focused on its pervasive spread and our strategies for keeping it at bay as much. As an anthropologist, I am inclined to understand how PEOPLE are making sense of this world, as we know it in the current circumstances of the COVID-19 pandemic. As a missiologist, I am interested in the implications of the disease on God's concern, and call to redeem PEOPLE in a broken world to order and justice.

We would also imagine that since people are on the top of the earth's food chain, most intelligent of all creatures and most technologically advanced, that it would be obvious to recognize our power and exercise it well. Power refers to privileges, opportunities, and influential statuses that people are endowed with. Power is a gift from God to all humans as bearers of his image. Because of the POWER bestowed to us, we are able to make sense of the world and exercise the duty of caring, subduing, and ruling it. Presumably, with this power, we can wage war on a virus because we have the ability to scientifically identify it, name it and exterminate it. We can also exercise our influences to make decisions that cause human thriving and empower others.

Yet sadly, power can be exercised badly, even hurtfully. Sometimes we may not be aware that our power is hurting others or causing injustice to others. This pandemic has brought to light some persistent power differentials in the world. For instance, the hype of 'flatten the curve' is about what power (in terms of health capacity) a country has to sufficiently deal with rising COVID-19 infections. Whether countries like it or not they are forced to count hospital beds, health care workers, the size of the treasury for contingencies; people are forced to scrutinize their own capacity to survive; and development agents and leaders are forced to examine their capacity in supporting the poor people in underserved communities. As a matter of fact, all people hold some form of relative power. Even those that are considered 'powerless' hold a latent potential to exercise the weapons of the weak as their power.

Focusing on people (men and women) as the core unit of society, we are drawn to ask: How will the different privileges and circumstances of men and women play out with reality of COVID-19? How will the decisions of the powerful influence others? How will existing inequalities play-out in the new norms that the pandemic has forced us to embrace? In this article, it is impossible to analyze the question of power in all these spheres. I will limit this to a narrower scope guided by emerging news on what is happening to/with people in these extraordinary days.

What is happening to PEOPLE?

- Increasing domestic violence.

- Thefts and petty crimes on the rise in the cities

- The vulnerabilities of those living in refugee camps and on the streets rising.

- School closures may mean some children will not return to school at all.

- Increased need for water exposes women to danger as they walk for long distances looking for water

- Early forced marriages to reduce burden on families reported

- Containment and lockdown have complicated the lives of those living with physical disabilities, street families, and the elderly.

- Attacks on the vulnerable during curfew enforcement

- Risk of re-infections

- Search for food by underserved communities such as slums create opportunities for exploitation

- Mental health problems on the rise

What has power got to do with these reports?

These issues affecting people and their lives are many. To adequately examine how power dynamics influences come to play, a framework is necessary. I propose what I call COVID-19 Oriented Gender Analysis (CO-GA) for that. Universally, Gender Analysis assesses men's and women's lives in relation to a given matter of reference and applies this in understanding policy, response or service delivery. Gender analysis provides a framework for holistic examination of differences between men and women's circumstances that may have implications on any intervention. It also looks at different levels of power held by men and women, different limitations and opportunities and how these affect their lives. CO-GA, which explores power dynamics within family, community and health-care systems is necessary for robust response. A broad review of reports, existing realities, news and observations reveal the following findings:

1. How will the different levels of power held by men and women affect how men and women access health care and adopt safety guidelines?

    a. Men more likely to play macho with safety guidelines such as failing to wear facemasks.

    b. Women less able to access mother and child care due to travel decisions

    c. Men are more likely to take risks – higher rate of COVID-19 in men has been noted

    d. Men more likely to play macho with safety guidelines such as failing to wear facemasks.

2. How will the lockdowns and containment restrictions affect men and women's work, health seeking behavior and general wellbeing?

    a. Women's triple work burden (reproductive roles, productive roles and community roles) will be intensified by added role of supervising children's school work occasioned by school closures

    b. Loss of jobs and pay cuts will affect both men and women's health seeking capabilities for existing health problems

    c. Stress and anxiety occasioned by COVID-19 will drive domestic violence. Women are more likely to be victims of rape/violence as men try to reclaim their threatened ability to provide for their families.

3. What roles do men and women have in allocation of COVID-19 resources?

    a. Men have more opportunities for participation in extra-domestic community initiatives where decisions on allocation of resources are made

    b. Women's domestic roles bar them from important information regarding available COVID-19 essential resource/supplies.

4. How are women and men's existing health care needs affected differently by COVID-19 response?

    a. More resources including human resources (health care workers) are allocated to COVID response thereby reducing attention on existing maternal and child health – for women, and management of other illnesses for both men an women.

5. How is the COVID-19 care delivery planned to meet special needs of men and women?

    a. Are isolation centres, quarantine centres organized with special needs of men and women in mind

Other Existing Realities

Troublesome Triple Roles: These preliminary realities are highlighted within an already growing evidence of domestic violence with lockdowns and containments. While domestic violence is more explicit problem that can be easily noted and reported, other problems rooted in cultural and social factors are also prevalent. These include triple work burdens, the reproductive, productive, and community roles (C. O. N. Moser 1993) by women have been intensified by the COVID-19 threatening to tip mental health problems and family disputes. Reproductive roles of child care, nurture and all other duties that support that such as supervising school work, cleaning, cooking, etc., have increased.

Before the pandemic's instigated lockdowns and containments, most of the productive work was carried out in the offices and outside of the home but now women are faced with the slippery task of trying to do it all in the same space and concurrently. To say the least, this situation is a ripe ground for anxiety, mental overload, and physical exhaustion that can compromise mental health. Responding to this will require individual family awareness on the risks and a determination by men to share these burdens for the good of the family.

Men's Livelihoods Burdens: Furthermore, this time has also drawn attention to existing gendering practices with effects on both men and women. For men, there is the normative expectation to lead the family and to provide for basic needs. This expectation brings about pressure but also risk taking moves that may endanger families. With job cuts, loss of businesses, and jobs, the very essence of masculinity for many men has been threatened. They cannot exercise confident leadership when many things are uncertain and unpredictable. Some choose compensating behaviors that are harmful such as alcohol and drugs.

Other studies on livelihood instabilities have shown that domestic violence are a result of threatened masculinities – men trying to compensate for their authority through wife battering (Amuyunzu-Nyamongo and Francis 2006; Thamari-Odhiambo 2018) In addition, these gendered norms in regard to men put them at risk of mental illness and reduced immunity to fight off other diseases.

Women's Femininity Mirage: Women also face a different but related gendered expectation to exercise acceptable femininity. Expectations to be exhibit 'proper' or accepted traits of femininity include: a proper woman should be calm, cool and collected; should maintain a clean home all the time; should not complain when tired; should look neat and smart all the time; should act confident etc. These expectations touch on important social roles such of motherhood, 'proper' wife, or 'proper' woman more generally. All these are culturally determined and put heavy pressure on women's mental, physical and psychological health. They create unattainable goals that increase anxiety. In time of crisis like we are in, new sets of expectations such as ability to teach own children, make meals, deliver on work targets and be a good wife make a new gauge of measuring 'properness.' This scenario is a ripe ground for new health challenges.

Why are men more at risk?

At the point of writing this in mid-April 2020, more men were leading in total number of infections and deaths than women. In United Kingdom for instance about 70% critically sick people were reported to be men. A higher number of infections among men had also been noted in China and in Africa. Medical and biological reasons for this have been offered. A study by Harvard Health Journal refuted the claim that smoking which is more prevalent in men predisposes lung cells to viral infection (Ball 2020). They argued instead that women have stronger immunity than men attributed to hormonal differences.

A factor of men being less hygienic and therefore being more likely to pick and carry viruses has also been offered. From a social anthropological point of view, however, the risk-taking nature of men and their out-of-home nature of work expose them to the virus. Women are also more likely to adhere to safety precautions by nature of their socialization than men. For instance, in one of isolation centres in Nairobi, men had been reported to have run away through the fence in blatant disregard of isolation guidelines.

People and Pay: Data from WHO shows that women form about 70% of workers in health and social sector. In Africa most male, 72% make up the workforce as physicians, pharmacists and dentists while women make 38% in those spaces. On the other end, women make a majority in nursing and midwifery, 65% while men represent 35% (Boniol et al. 2019). This is a good indication of women's participation in these sectors but there is a reported 11% of gendered pay gap. This means that on average, with same qualifications and working in the same job roles, men earn 11% more than women (Boniol et al. 2019). The demand of COVID-19 pandemic puts a spotlight on these existing inequalities thereby necessitating a return to the ILO'S recommended gender equity policies. The ILO's remuneration recommendation states that countries should endeavor to "ensure the application to all workers of the principle of equal remuneration for men and women workers for work of equal value."

Conclusion

To fight this pandemic and cross over to the other side of history, we must see PEOPLE as the lens through which intervene and understand the emerging issues. The virus is here and has ravaged our economy and social fabric immensely; shall we them still let it take our humanity? We must be people-centric, we must ask questions of history – how did the past pandemic affect people, their work, and families? We must ask justice questions – How can we sharpen our mantra for a just world through the experiences of this pandemic? We must then ask the power questions? How are the differences of men and women's privileges and existing structures and circumstances going to affect our response to COVID-19?

Here is a suggested beginning point:

For each of the key contexts of action namely Health and Policy; Government agencies; NGO's and religious communities and Family and individual contexts, a COVID-19 oriented Gender Analysis (CO-GA) is outlined in the framework below. Recommendation for people-centred lens to all actions and suggestions of indicators of impact beyond those actions are also highlighted.

CO-GA & Recommendations for action	Impact/ outcome indicators
Health policy and systems	
1. Beware of cultural practices and norms that negatively affect health-seeking behaviour by men and women.	1. Health care workers, contact tracing teams aware of men and women's health-seeking behaviors
2. Provide frameworks for ensuring other critical existing health needs are not neglected	2. Other critical health needs continue to be addressed

3. Provide equal and timely remuneration of health care workers 4. Provide guidelines for psychosocial care for doctors and nurses on the front line.	3. Equitable remuneration of health care workers 4. Health care workers who are emotionally an mentality healthy
Government Agencies	
1. Ensure collection of gender and age disaggregated data for targeted interventions 2. Provide rescue mechanism and safe centres for those affected by gender based violence (GBV) 3. De-bunk myths about COVID-19 using trusted and culturally sensitive forums.	1. Availability of gender and age disaggregated data 2. Rescue mechanism of GBV victims in place 3. Clear and factual Information disseminated through trusted community forums

NGO's and religious communities	
1. Utilize existing social groups for awareness and information sharing – recognize the value of affinity groups in care for the sick. 2. Ensure provision of essential health products such as SRHR services and sanitary products as part of essential services and products. 3. Provide safe centres for those affected by GBV 4. Provide essential basic supplies to the poor and the vulnerable and ensure men and women are involved in distribution decisions	1. Clear and factual Information disseminated through existing social groups 2. Reproductive health services provided and sanitary products included as essential relief item. 3. Victims of GBV have safe centres for counselling and rehabilitation 4. Essential basic supplies distributed to the needy

5. Create awareness on power dynamics that cause people discrimination such as stigma related to pre-existing conditions and status that may hinder access to equal healthcare	5. Awareness of stigmatizing myths and no stigma on the affected.
Individual and Family level	
1. Talk about cultural attitudes that drive risks and restrict men and women from seeking health care 2. Create awareness on work burdens and share them to prevent overload and mental health risks on overworked family members	1. Reduced health risks due to individuals and families awareness of cultural attitudes that drive risks. 2. Reduced mental overload

In conclusion, let the people-centric view be the lens through which we reflect, act and respond to this pandemic. The clinical aspects of response are clear-cut focusing on the virus. Let our humanity draw us to look beyond this virus to PEOPLE. CO-GA offers an illustrative beginning point for that.

"I have seen the affliction of my PEOPLE. I have heard their cry of distress. Yes, I am aware of their suffering." (Exodus 3:7)

REFERENCES

Amuyunzu-Nyamongo, Mary, and Paul Francis. 2006. "Collapsing Livelihoods and the Crisis of Masculinity in Rural Kenya." In The Other Half of Gender. Washington D.C: World Bank Publications.

Ball, Philip. 2020. "Coronavirus Hits Men Harder: Here Is What Scientists Know about It." The Guardian, April 7, 2020, sec. Opinion: Coronavirus Outbreak. https://www.theguardian.

com/commentisfree/2020/apr/07/coronavirus-hits-men-harder-evidence-risk.

Boniol, Matthew, Michelle McIsaac, Lihui Xu, Tana Wuliji, Khassoum Diallo, and Jimm Campbell. 2019. "Gender Equity in the Health Workforce: Analysis of 104 Countries." WHO. https://apps.who.int/iris/bitstream/handle/10665/311314/WHO-HIS-HWF-Gender-WP1-2019.1-eng.pdf.

Moser, Caroline O. N. 1993. Gender Planning and Development: Theory, Practice, and Training. London ; New York: Routledge.

Thamari-Odhiambo, Mary. 2018. "Widow Cleansing in Rural Kenya: Toward a Critically Contextualized Theological Response." In African Contextual Realities. S.l.: Langham Global Library.

Leading Organizational Change in the Context of COVID-19

Dr Joshua Wathanga, Consultant in Policy, Strategy, and Governance

Covid-19 Pandemic in Context

Not since the Spanish Flu pandemic a century ago, which claimed more than 50 million lives, has humankind faced the magnitude of a global crisis like Covid-19. We must pray that the coronavirus pandemic does not devastate a fraction of the Spanish flu toll, but regardless, this crisis will change the world, as we know it. Even a brief analysis of the political, economic, social, technological, environmental, and legal (PESTEL) shows that the effects of the pandemic, and the decisions people and governments are taking and will take in the weeks and months ahead, will shape the world for years. In a recent newspaper article, Professor X.N. Iraki (2020) postulates that the politics of the future will change depending on how governments handle the pandemic and a closer examination of the efficacy of democracy versus other forms of governance. Is it possible that the more effective handling of the crisis by Asian countries has something to do with authoritarian regimes? How come otherwise 'advanced' economies of Western nations have been more devastated by this pandemic?

Economically, the pandemic will have devastating consequences brought by direct and indirect costs of medical interventions, business interruption locally and for export, and near stand-still tourist, entertainment, airline industries, just to mention a few. Socially, lockdowns have brought us closer physically to our families, but have not necessarily made us better friends as evidenced by a rise in domestic violence thus highlighting the societies' deeper ills. Perhaps one boon of the pandemic is ecological with the earth getting a much-needed sabbatical for renewal with the reduction of greenhouse gases (Environmental Protection, 2020) though the effect may be short-lived depending on the interventions we choose to mitigate the disruptions (World Bank, 2020). It would appear that going forward, one of the greatest impacts of the pandemic is technological. Positively, learning to work remotely as efficiently, if not more, than face-to-face is likely to define the workplace, and especially education, for good. This of course has huge consequences for work and Church ministry that require more face-to-face interaction.

What is ominous though is the inevitable long arm of governments needing, but also taking advantage of, increased surveillance for purposes of, or in the guise of, controlling the epidemic. Prof. Yuval Noah Harari (2020) traces the history of surveillance during past crises to warn about what we should expect going into the future. Giving of an illustration of China, Harari states, "By closely monitoring people's smartphones, making use of hundreds of millions of face-recognizing cameras, and obliging people to check and report their body temperature and medical condition, the Chinese authorities can not only quickly identify suspected coronavirus carriers, but also track their movements and identify anyone they came into contact with." We would be naïve to think that this Orwellian 'Brave New World' is limited to only China!

Change: The New Normal

The socio-economic effects of Covid-19 are going to be with us much longer than the pandemic itself, and are likely to redefine our present and future for many years to come. If you are a leader or aspire to be one, you need to get used to the changes that this crisis will bring to you personally and for your organization or ministry. It is not just about the coronavirus crisis, but organizations are operating in increasingly complex, and fast changing environments in which an adaptation to the environmental changes is an imperative.

Change is necessary if organizations are to survive and thrive in constantly changing internal and external environment. Even before Covid-19 pandemic, the external world had become complex and competitive and every organization has to reconceptualize every aspect of how they do business to meet changing needs of customers. The external world is constantly changing and organizations must keep up with the political, economic, social, technological, environmental and legal (Pestel) developments that may have implications for their particular business. Even national armies are finding that they have to undergo massive changes in order to fight a new kind of war and replace all-out assault and use of force to the use of counter-insurgency intelligence (Serena, 2011). Change is the constant and stability the exception, and as Mark Twain puts it, "A round man cannot be expected to fit into a square hole right away. He must have time to modify his shape."

Most definitions of leadership include change and transformation and it is now recognized as the essence of leadership. If you are not transforming yourself you are standing still is fast becoming the new mantra (Financial Review, 2019). The pressing need for change management is reflected in the fact that many companies are hiring transformation officers who are charged with radically rethinking and remaking either the entire organization or parts of it (FTI Consulting, 2020). The leader of the future will not only have to anticipate change, but has to thrive on it. Says Tom Peters (1987) in the preface of his book "Thriving on Chaos": "The winners of tomorrow will deal proactively with chaos, will look at the chaos per se as the source of market advantage, not a problem to be got around. Chaos and uncertainty are (will be) market opportunities for the wise; capitalizing on fleeting market anomalies will be the successful business's greatest accomplishment."

The Covid-19 crisis is, at the very least, going to lay bare the fact that our traditional models of leadership are not effective and we need to develop leaders who are more comfortable with the transformation process. Organizational leaders of the present and the future must face new challenges in a changing environment which is referred to as VUCA, which stands for volatility, uncertainty, complexity and ambiguity. The organizations that want to succeed will have to reinvent themselves and transform under the leadership of new leaders or those willing to change. According to Professor Juan Carlos Pastor (2018), transformational leaders need five competencies if the change process in their organizations is going to last. First, they need to be system thinkers who see the big picture and where the organization is going. Second, they have to be authentic and inspire trust of their teams. Third, they must inspirational; passion is contagious and leaders must provide meaning through leading by example. Fourth, transformational leaders must think outside the box and promote innovation, and finally, leaders must coach and develop people, skills, and structures so that the change process lasts for a long time.

Navigating the Impact of Covid-19 on your Organization

The coronavirus pandemic is such a huge disrupter that it is going to change the world in all its PESTEL dimensions. If the world is going to change, so will your organization! So, what tools do leaders need in order to navigate the new chaos and complexity visited upon by Covid-19 and other changes that will face our organizations, ministries, and businesses?

1. Clarify your Core Purpose

Just as it is important for each individual not to go through life without seeking to know the purpose for which we were created, each organization must be clear about its reason for existence. As Professor Nicholas Pearce (2019) puts it in his book, "The Purpose Path", all the questions we ask of ourselves can also be asked of organizations: What is our purpose? Who are we? What are we here for? What is success for us? Are we good citizens? Are we doing it ethically? Many organizations can easily follow the allure of "success" to become what they're not designed to be. One of the effects of Covid-19 is that it will force us to ask questions of why our organizations exist so that we can do better what we are meant to do and leave those additional responsibilities we have picked along the way.

Mission creep happens when an organization strays beyond the original mission of the organization. It's very easy to do subconsciously and often occurs after an organization or ministry sees some success of their own and wants to extend the success to areas that were not originally in the plan- all with great intentions. For example, there are many churches that have schools, rental properties, farms, development departments, to mention just a few. A number of these initiatives, of course, are either directly connected to the ministry of the church for outreach and resource mobilization purposes, but we need to be careful to avoid losing focus on the real purpose of the organization. Four things can help you avoid mission creep, namely (The A Group, 2019): find your niche; be clear about your mission; learn to say "no"; and, use your mission as a filter for decision-making.

2. Adopt a Growth Mindset

The Covid-19 pandemic is also going to expose whether as leaders we have a growth or fixed mindsets. According to research by world-renowned Stanford University psychologist, Dr. Carol Dweck (2016), leaders with a fixed mindset believe that skills and abilities are born and finite and that you can't learn or grow. On the other hand, a growth-mindset leader believes that skills can be built and abilities developed, and so you can learn and grow throughout life. The impact of these two types of leaders during a crisis is very different: Fixed mindset leaders have no time for mistakes as they interpret them as failure, and so they back down and try to avoid challenging situations. Such leaders are also very sensitive to negative feedback, which they take personally and defensively. Refreshingly, growth mindset leaders take mistakes as a learning opportunity and so they embrace new challenges and welcome feedback as a chance to learn and develop. The good news from this research is that we can all develop a growth mindset by envisioning positive outcomes while leading in crisis and reframing failure as a chance to learn.

3. Lead rather than Manage

In crisis situations, especially those as fluid as the coronavirus outbreak, leaders may be inclined to manage their team's response, leaving staff over-managed and under-led. In a recent Harvard Business Review written with coronavirus pandemic in mind, McNulty and Marcus (2020) opine that crises, replete with both complexity and change, require executives to both lead and manage effectively. Addressing the urgent needs of the present is the work of management. You need to make immediate choices and allocate resources. The pace is fast, and actions are decisive. Leading, by contrast, involves guiding people to the best possible eventual outcome over this arc of time. Your focus needs to be on what is likely to come next and readying to meet it. That means seeing beyond the immediate to anticipate the next three, four, or five obstacles. There is nothing as disconcerting for team members than a leader who is only strong on tasks and micro-manages activities, without giving them the big picture of where the organization is heading and how to get there.

4. Effective Decision-Making

Your leadership mettle will be put to severe test by a crisis such as Covid-19 especially if you had not established a good working relationship with your team members. An important factor that determines the style applied by a leader is the extent to which he or she is focused on demonstrating concern for employee welfare. It is therefore necessary for the leader to create social relations with the employees and take advantage of them, and this is achieved by providing feedback, being helpful, listening to complaints, being friendly and treating employees as equals (Cappelen Damm As, 2010). Seeking views and information and listening carefully to what team members are saying is very important for effective decision-making, but the leader still has to do their job in making decisions that only they can make.

Our understanding of leadership styles has been transformed by the work of Daniel Goleman, Richard Boyatzis, and Annie McKee (2002) who have described six distinct emotional leadership styles. Each of these styles has a different effect on people's emotions, and each has strengths and weaknesses in different situations. Four of these styles (Authoritative, Coaching, Affiliative, and Democratic) promote harmony and positive outcomes, while two styles (Coercive and Pacesetting) can create tension, and should only be used in specific situations. Goleman and his co-authors say that no one style should be used all of the time. Instead, the six styles should be used interchangeably, depending on the specific needs of the situation and the people that you're dealing with.

5. Adapt to the New Reality

We need to be clear that coronavirus is not a 'passing cloud' and it is going nowhere; it is a new disruptive pathogen that is going to be with us for a long time. Its socio-economic effects are going to last much longer and will be bigger than the pandemic, and so we need to move away from a post-Covid-19 mindset and adapt to it (Ndii, 2020). We noted in the context analysis of this pandemic that every area will change: in politics, economics, socially, technology, legally, and ecologically.

How are you going to adapt to the new reality your

organization will be operating under? Having clarified your core-purpose, do you need to shed goals and activities that are not consistent with your mission? Are there unnecessary overhead costs that you can do away with? What of maximizing on innovation and technology for greater effectiveness and productivity? How will you ensure you have the "right people in the bus" and you invest in them for their development and productivity? As Jim Collins (2001) puts it, "leaders of companies that go from good to great start not with "where" but with "who." They start by getting the right people on the bus, the wrong people off the bus, and the right people in the right seats."

BIBLIOGRAPHY

Achua, C. F. (2013). Effective Leadership (5th ed.). South-Western, Cengage.

Beckman, J. (2000, October). Religion in Post-World War II America. Retrieved April 20, 2020 from National Humanities' Centre: http://nationalhumanitiescenter.org/tserve/twenty/tkeyinfo/trelww2.htm

Brown, J. (n.d.). From https://www.brainyquote.com/quotes/h_jackson_brown_jr_134502

Buechner, F. (2017, July 18). From https://www.frederickbuechner.com/quote-of-the-day/2017/7/18/vocation

Buford, B. (2008). Halftime: Moving from Success to Significance. Grand Rapids, Michigan: Zondervan.

Collins, J. (2001). Good to Great. New York: Harper Collins.

Curtis, H. D. (2011). God is Not Affected by the Great Depression. Pentecostal Missions During the 1930s , 80 (3), 579-589.

Dweck, C. (2016). Mindset: The New Psychology of Success. New York : Penguin Random House.

Environmental Protection. (2020, March 24). COVID-19 and Climate Change: The Unexpected Pairing. Environmental Protection. From https://eponline.com/articles/2020/03/24/covid19-and-climate-change-the-unexpected-pairing.aspx

Financial Review. (2019, February 28). Transformation Officers Replace Consultants.

Ford, H. (n.d.). From http://www.ft.lk/columns/surround-yourself-with-the-best-people-you-can-find/4-69735

FTI Consulting. (2020). The Rise of the Transformation Officer. FTI Consulting.

Gatu, J. (2006). Joyfully Christian and Joyfully African. Nairobi: Acton.

Goleman, D. (1996). Emotional Intelligence: Why it Can Matter More Than IQ. Bloomsbury.

Goleman, D. (2004, January). What Makes a Leader? Harvard Business Review , 1-10.

Goleman, D., Boyatzis, R., & McKee, A. (2002). Primal Leadership: Realizing the Power of Emotional Intelligence. Harvard Business Review.

Harari, Y. N. (2020, March 20). The World After Coronavirus. Financial Times. From https://www.ft.com/content/19d90308-6858-11ea-a3c9-1fe6fedcca75

Iraki, X. N. (2020, April 6). A Glimpse into Post Coronavirus World. From https://www.standardmedia.co.ke/article/2001366881/a-glimpse-into-post-coronavirus-world

Leipzig, A. (2013, February 1). How to Know Your Life Purpose in 5 Minutes. From https://youtu.be/vVsXO9brK7M?list=PL5qZYippVH6nQWgF4jhUOZEAPRsx0df_A

Luther, M. (1955). Advice in Time of Epidemic and Famine. In M. Luther, & T. G. Tappert (Ed.), Letters of Spiritual Counsel (pp. 228-257). Westminster: Westminster Press.

Maxwell, J. C. (2003, January 3). Leadership 101.

McNulty, E., & Marcus, L. (2020, March 25). Are you Leading Through Crisis or Managing the Response? Harvard Business Review .

Ndii, D. (2020, April 28). COVID-19 and the Economy. Royal Media Services. Citizen TV, Nairobi.

Noll, M. A. (2012). Turning Points: Decisive Moments in the History of Christianity (3rd ed.). Grand Rapids, Michigan: Baker Academic.

Palmer, P. J. (2000). Let Your Life Speak: Listening for the Voice of Vocation. John Wiley & Sons, Inc.

Pastor, J. C. (Composer). (2018). Five Characteristics of the Transformational Leader. IE University.

Pearce, N. (2019). The Purpose Path: A Guide to Pursuing Your Authentic Work. New York: St Martin's Press.

Peters, T. (1987). Thriving on Chaos: Handbook for a Management Revolution. Harper Collins.

Piper, J. (2020). Coronavirus and Christ. Wheaton, IL: Crossway.

Selart, M. (2010). A leadership Perspective on Decision Making. Cappelen Damm As.

Serena, C. C. (2011). A Revolution in Military Adaptation: The US Army in the Iraq War. Washington DC: Georgetown University Press. Washington DC: Georgetown University Press.

Shaw, M. (2010). Global Awakening: How 20th Century Revivals Triggered a Christian Revolution. Downers Grove, Illinois: IVP Academic.

Stark, R. (1997). The Rise of Christianity: How the Obscure, Marginal Jesus Movement Became the Dominant Religious Force in the Western World in a Few Centuries. San-Francisco: Harper.

The A Group. (2019, September 25). 4 Ways to Avoid Mission Creep. From https://www.agroup.com/blog/4-ways-to-avoid-mission-creep/

Wallace, A. F. (2003). Revitalization Movements. In R. S. Grumet (Ed.), Revitalizations and Mazeways. Lincoln, Nebraska: University of Nebraska.

Warren, R. (1997). What am I Here For? The Purpose Driven Life. Zondervan.

World Bank. (2020, April 22). Earth Day 2020: Could COVID-19 Be the Tipping Point for Transport Emissions? From https://www.worldbank.org/en/news/feature/2020/04/22/earth-day-2020-could-covid-19-be-the-tipping-point-for-transport-emissions

Yeomans, S. (2017). The Antonine PLague and the Spread of Christianity. Biblical Archaeology Review , 43, 24-66.

Post-COVID Dreams: Aspirations for Social-Economic Justice

By Mary Thamari, PhD

How can one see beyond the mist?
How do you dream in the dark of the tunnel?
Where is the light?
Do sight in the dark tunnel rely on light alone?
Can darkness can shine a light of it's own?

Some special light?

This pandemic has pulled out a dark cloud akin to wading through murky effluent in a dark tunnel without an end in sight. In reality, this darkness might be a blessing in disguise. Deep thoughts and dreams are often incubated in the darkness of closed eyes or stillness of silence. When we close our eyes to darkness, we shake off the light that can disrupt the flow. We allow stillness and targeted focus. The darkness that is COVID-19 has exposed many injustices that we would not have seen in the 'brighter' times before. We now see the social injustices that the society has managed to keep well tucked under wraps. Thankfully, we are able to have clearer aspirations of what we would want to see beyond COVID-19. I focus my attention on three key social-economic spaces as lens through which I lay out post-COVID-19 aspirations: The health care systems, the education sector and the livelihoods statuses of the vulnerable. What we have has been a health care system that is ineffective and insufficient, an unequal education landscape and a fragile livelihood means for many.

Health Sector Realities in Kenya

The state of health care systems has been a topic of public debate and negotiations for long. When Kenyan medical doctors went on strike a few years back, they agitated for improved provision of health care resources, improved health management systems and increased health care workers to meet the demand for ordinary health needs in the country. The reality could not be better expressed by words of one young mother, "when my child is sick, I need to choose whether to go to daktari or to buy food. What would you do in my case?" This is a knee gelling question in a scene where many, a majority, who live by the daily wage would be contending. Patients sharing hospital beds and nurses' exhaustion due to unmanageable patients characterize many public hospitals. These problems seem to be the problem of only those who couldn't access boutique clinics in private hospitals. Yet, those who can afford are the main custodians of decision-making power on health care matters. Is it a wonder then that these public hospitals where the poor go have remained in poor state for eons? A World Bank report indicated that Kenyan doctors have a high rate of absenteeism in public health facilities indicating poor efficiency in public hospital as compared to private hospitals.

Anecdotal media reports of patients dying on queues waiting for medical attention, father's smuggling their children out of hospitals unable to pay and pregnant mothers dying on long treks to deliver babies, have exposed this rancid state. COVID-19 has highlighted this stark reality. The cross-boarder closures by many countries means that no one can seek medical care elsewhere. The same hospitals that have been neglected will be needed to fight the disease and to treat other illnesses. No more medical airlifts by the powerful, at least for the time. This and the reality of what we have now to do with is a sobering, but also shameful. That we can be comfortable in word where a basic health necessity like sanitary towels is inaccessible to young school girls, where a father has to choose sneaking away from hospital due to unpaid bills and where patients share beds in hospitals – is utterly unacceptable!

A few days before writing this this article, a group of medical doctors and nurses had staged a disapproval strike in one of the Kenyan counties protesting non-payment of their dues – they alleged that the county government had not paid for months. This was a jaw-dropping scenario to imagine that people involved in daily risk of fighting a pandemic and other existing diseases had not been paid for so long. They also complained of lack of personal protective equipment (PPE).

 Yet, this very disgraceful and unacceptable situation can be good fodder for our aspirational re-imagination of a relatively just, accessible and effective health care system. Studies have shown that although the WHO recommended doctor patient ratio is 1 doctor to 1000 patients, Kenya's current ratio is 1:17000. As far as health financing is concerned, Kenya ranks 140 out of 190 in WHO World's Health Systems Ranking (Tandon et al. 2000). According to the Abuja Declaration by AU states, the recommended budget allocation for health is 15% of the total budget (WHO 2011). Kenya's 2018/2019 budget allocation to health was about 9.2% (Health Policy Plus 2019). Granted that part of health functions were devolved and some budget committed to county governments, the evident needs in health sector still require attention.

Areas such as health research, development of health technologies, training and deployment of health care workers and provision of essential medical infrastructure requires an improved budget commitment.

Aspirations for Health Care

1. A robust universal health care for all targeting those who are already facing multiple economic stressors. I dream of a time when no will have to choose between food and health care.

2. Improved accessibility to health care facilities. I dream of a time when no woman will give birth on the way side or die walking for long distances to deliver precious life.

3. Increased training and deployment of health care workers. I dream of decongested hospital halls, non-stressed doctors and where no one dies queuing.

4. Improved provision of medical supplies, equipment and improved technology to ease diagnosis and management of patients. I dream of a time when no one will have to travel outside the country to seek medical care. I dream of a time where no one will have to be dismissed from hospital without medication.

Education Realities in Kenya

The measures taken to mitigate the spread of COVID-19 have included school closures, a move that has many implications on education. The already existing inequalities have been heightened by the closures. A few months ago, there was a spotlight on proliferation of poorly-built schools all over the country. This was preceded by a collapse of a school in one of Nairobi's informal settlements that led to the death of 7 pupils and injury of about 50. This tragedy was followed by an onslaught on proprietors of these kinds of schools and what many considered as greed and lack of compassion for the poor children. Little attention was directed to WHY this kind of situation exists in the first place.

Why would a parent take their well-loved child to a shanty private school, and not to a public school? Why would a businessperson choose a school project for income generation? Why do the majority of the poor living in slums accept the conditions of such schools? The answer to these questions takes us to the often hidden realities in what seems to be a well-organized education delivery system in the country. While the software or the content of education may seem okay – a syllabus, the hardware or the vehicle of its delivery is lacking. Children in shanty schools are expected to go through the same curriculum as children in well-resourced schools and later compete on the same economic space. I had the privilege of volunteering to teach in one of the shanty schools for 2 lessons a week in one of Nairobi's slums. My intention was to zoom in my ethnographic lens in order to understand the realities and how to best intervene. This time revealed the undying aspirational dreams carried by parents when they deliver their children to any school. One of the parents of the children in my grade 2 class was a young mother who used to sell tea at the Railway station every evening. She used every penny she earned to feed her 2 children and nothing much to save for their education. So, this school became a place of hope—a place she could anchor her dreams for a better future. She represented many.

The poorly resourced schools exist because there is a gap

– there are far few public schools to take in all school-going children. Is this something the state does not know? The demographic data does provide projections for population growth and corresponding social facilities such as schools to meet that demand. In the current state of affairs, then parents have no choice but to take their children to dangerous learning spaces such as the one that collapsed.

These children in city's informal settlements and in other poorly resourced places in the country also face the risk of school dropouts in the wake of COVID-19 school closures. Many children are attracted and retained in these schools by school-feeding programs. Without these, some may get into risky food-earning mechanisms – petty theft or even commercial sex work. In some places there have been reports of early marriages as families try to ease the burden of care. A post-COVID survey on effects of closures may reveal more than we see now.

Technology has been acclaimed as the complementary to learning during the lockdown. However, few have access to infrastructure required to learn and to effectively engage online learning platforms. The injustice of multiple deprivations, marginalization and exploitation of poor and vulnerable populations has been more amplified by this pandemic. Yet, this provides an opportunity to aspire for a just education management systems.

Aspirations for Education Sector

1. Increased and improved public schools. So no parent will have to present their child to a school-entrepreneur who cares more about profits than child welfare. I dream of a time when parents who live with multiple vulnerabilities will have hope because their children are getting quality education

in proper learning facilities like any other child. I hope to see a day when the poor and the rich children can meet in the same learning space and get equal and quality education.

2. Improved training and deployment of teachers. So no child is subjected to untrained incompetent teachers for lack of alternatives. I dream of a time when teachers will not have to teach 100 children in one room.

3. Increased provision of education facilities and resources such as books, computers and learning aids. So all children can explore learning unhindered and having no worry about lacking writing material or a workbook. I dream of school spaces with story books, science books, arts books and all manner of books so children can explore as much as they can. I dream of learning spaces that are not a danger to children and where they can learn to reimagine the kind of homes they would like to have for themselves.

Fragile Livelihoods

The pandemic has also revealed the fragility of livelihoods. There has been job losses, pay cuts, and business losses. Within a day after Kenya's president pronounced a curfew in the country, there were numerous distress calls and lamentations over business losses. There had been actions by some employers, cutting pay or giving unpaid leave to employees – a move to survive the uncertain period. In a country where informal sector is the mainstay for many, attention has been drawn to this fragile yet significant economic space.

One of the characteristics of informal sector is their

unprotected and unregulated mode of operations (ILO). The dualist school of thought sees this sector as having no relationship with the formal sector and see it as peripheral initiatives that offer income to the poor. However, the structuralist school of thought sees the informal sector as inherently connected to capitalist formal sector and as 'subordinated economic units' (Castells and Portes, 1989). The structuralist view that has received evidential support from many studies portend that informal sector is composed of the poor who are engaged in the subsistence initiatives on one end and lucrative ventures on the other end. While the poor on the bottom of the ladder earn below minimum wage, the others on top of the informal sector ladder earn substantially high wages (ILO 2000). The operations in this sector are fluid, unpredictable and vulnerable to social and economic shocks. This unpredictability has been intensified by uncertainties of COVID-19 pandemic.

The rise of the informal sector as a way to understand economic activity came about in a particular ideological and social-political context. In the 1950s and 1960s, developmentalist perspectives emerged in which development economists and political scientists theorized the need for all societies, especially those outside of North America and Europe, to move from being traditional to being modernized or developed (Chen et al., 2004; Reddock, 2000). Urbanization, the growth of industries, regulated labour and the creations of jobs were together envisioned as the trajectory of development that would lead to an expansion in waged employment. But, on the contrary, unemployment, poor pay for the employed, and the proliferation of slums in urban centres became a common pattern across Africa.

Widespread unemployment raised concerns in the

developing world, which led to the commissioning of the International Labour Office (ILO) to investigate the phenomenon in Kenya, Sri Lanka and Colombia (C. Moser 1978). From the research mission, there was evidence of growth in both secure and insecure activities (ILO, 1972). In Kenya, the mission found that unemployment was linked to imbalances in opportunities for work and a lack of those opportunities overall (ILO, 1972: ix). In addition, low incomes in self-employment and waged work were identified as a growing trend of the working poor (ILO, 1972:1, 9). The informal sector therefore came to be understood as an all-encompassing category referring to the working poor in urban centres, those in unregulated self-employment, and low wage employment in insecure jobs (Hope, 2014:). Chen et al., 2004; Hope, 2012; Pahl, 1988).

Lack of regulation is due to limited understanding of the intricate workings of the sector and the costly regulatory regimes that workers cannot manage. Yet, this has particular effects on people's lives in the informal sector. For instance, there is little support from the government when it comes to basic social amenities such as health facilities and water and sanitation services in workspaces. For example there has been regular fire breakout in Kenya's largest market, Gikomba with hundreds of people loosing business. Wages are also low and uncertain, and workers have no safety protection. The employers, who contract informal sector workers on a day-to-day basis, remain the sole decision makers on rates of pay. In some way, it seems that informal sector has tuned to be a ripe place for exploitation of workers — an enclave for cheap labour! Because there are no binding obligations, as would be the case in regulated formal places of work, employer and employee relationships remain open to uncertain and often exploitative arrangements (Thamari 2019).

Dreams for the Fragile Livelihoods

1. Improved policies that support and encourage rural and urban informal sector. So many people can reach out to the potential of this sector not as a peripheral survivalist activity but a lucrative venture. I dream of a time when informal sector work will not be a last stop option but a top on the list option – absorbing many unemployed youth and building livelihoods for many.

2. Clear and enforceable regulations governing remuneration of workers in informal sector. So no one is exploited. I dream of a time when people will earn what they have sweated for and where they feel dignified by the pay they receive.

3. Well-serviced social amenities, water sanitation and hygiene facilities in markets to improve working conditions. So informal workers can stay clear of waterborne diseases and indignity of filth in their working spaces. I dreams of clean streets, clean air and conducive healthy work conditions.

4. Reduced existing constraints on access to affordable credit, and in-job training for informal sector workers. So informal workers can easily access credit and on-job training to improve their skills for work.

5. Improve policy and supply systems to increase access to inputs, technologies and equipment by informal sector workers. So that business can grow in breadth and in depth – earning better returns for workers

6. A well developed and coordinated insurance schemes for health and social security, so workers can work with a peace of mind and access health care when needed. I dream of a time when business will continue to thrive even when the proprietor falls ill.

May this pandemic sharpen our vision for a just world and may dreams incubated help anchor our actions for a flourishing world.

REFERENCES

Chen, Martha Alter, Joann Vanek, and Marilyn Carr. 2004. Mainstreaming Informal Employment and Gender in Poverty Reduction: A Handbook for Policy Makers and Othe Stakeholders. London: The Commonwealth Secretariat.

Health Policy Plus. 2019. "Kenya's Health Sector Budget: An Analysis of National and County Accounts for Fiscal Year 2018/2019." http://www.healthpolicyplus.com/ns/pubs/11306-11586_KenyaBudgetAnalysis.pdf.

Hope, Kempe Ronald. 2014. "Informal Economic Activity in Kenya: Its Benefits and Drawbacks." African Geographical Review 33 (1): 67–80.

Hope, Kempe Ronald, Sr. 2012. The Political Economy of Development in Kenya. Continuum International Publishing Group.

ILO. 1972. Employment, Incomes and Equality: A Strategy for Increasing Productive Employment in Kenya. Geneva: ILO.

Moser, Caroline. 1978. "Informal Sector or Petty Commodity Production: Dualism or Independence in Urban Development." World Development 6: 1041–64.

Pahl, R.E. 1988. "Some Remarks on Informal Work, Social Polarization and the Social Structure." International Journal of Urban and Regional Research 12 (2).

Reddock, Rhoda. 2000. "Why Gender? Why Development?" In Theoretical Perspectives on Gender and Development. IDRC.

Tandon, Ajay, Christopher JL. Murray, Jeremy A. Lauer, and David Evans. 2000. "Measuring Overall Health System Perfomance for 191 Countries." WHO. https://www.who.int/healthinfo/paper30.pdf.

WHO. 2011. "The Abuja Declaration: 10 Year On." World Health Organisation, Health Systems. 2011.

Reaffirming our Hope In God

By George Ogalo, National Director, FOCUS Kenya

Who can survive a life and a world that is not anchored in Hope?

There are only a few seasons when the world is united in seeking divine help on a matter. Corona virus has provided one such moment. A pandemic such as corona virus heightens our gasping for hope – hope both to survive and to thrive again. To be sure, God has always been connected to his world, reaffirming his acts of mercy and power. Individuals, organizations, and nations can always look up to God for his presence, his power, and his comfort! But this hope must be well-anchored on solid foundation.

It is not possible to fully account for **the burden of pandemics**, but the history of pandemics points to serious economic, social, and religious disruptions. Like the previous ones, Covid-19 comes with lingering unpredictability and uncertainty. In actual sense, Covid-19 may portend greater negative impact than previous pandemics. The previous pandemics did not have as much geographical scope neither occasioned by enhanced global movement. Neither did they happen within the same economic realities as it is today. The threat and prospects of economic storm recalls the 1930's great depression, and would further raise Covid-19 mark in world history. The challenge brought by the virus has different dimensions, including getting into the depths of despair.

Prior to Covid-19, the world is already tantalized and bearing the burden of adverse climate change whose consequences are beginning to overwhelm its inhabitants through heat waves, fires, floods, landslides, and the attendant illnesses related to compromised environment. However, nothing has tested global pandemic preparedness like Covid-19 because it's effect has been rapid and with multiple effects. Despite previous attempts to enhance preparedness by refining standards and raising funding levels to build health capacity, covid-19 has caught the world unawares, and disabused the notion that human beings can be fully prepared for any emerging pandemic. There are several aspects that rub in the concerns about the burden: experts have explained that the unique challenge that Covid-19 presents is the manner in which it mutates and spreads; resource constraints to contain the virus have been evident, even in countries perceived to have better healthcare infrastructure; and there are lingering possibilities of second, or even more waves of Covid-19 in countries that will have flattened the curves, especially as it turns out that the search for vaccines to contain covid-19 continues to be elusive or too slow. There are even concerns that finding the vaccine would be one good step, but acquiring the vaccine for the larger world population may lengthen the misery in some parts of the world. It is even grimmer to suggest, we pray not, that pandemics might be more frequent in the future because of factors such as increased urbanization, climate change, and globalization. One would, therefore, understand **the weight of leadership** and attendant frustrations in the efforts to counter the infection rate and offer healthcare to victims.

The initial shock of Corona virus emergence and spread

should be memorable. Within a short time, it dictated basic life protocols. The virus has dictated our personal social space, modes of interaction, and even worship. With no respect for existing class categories, it has been obvious that when world leaders keep distance and wear masks, it is not simply to demonstrate or model appropriate health behavior– they have been exercising protection regimes against the health threats to their personal lives by Covid-19. It has imposed on cultures new ways of greetings, burial procedures, travel arrangements, worship experiences, and many other demands never anticipated – almost resetting our social lives. It has placed both the rich and poor on the platform of beginning to only think about livelihood – food, shelter, and life itself. Ironically, Covid-19 has even occasioned a reversal of safe places. In Kenya, for example, the sick people have been hesitant to go for medical attention for fear of contracting the disease at the better health facilities; expectant parents are concerned about the timing of the Corona virus and their hopes for getting babies. For the first time airports and executive ports have been more unsafe than lonely village paths. On the economic and social front, it has disrupted both the employer and employees, and triggered survival conversations in families and communities. Men losing their jobs have felt emasculated for not only being confined, but also unable to feed their families. The net effect is that Covid-19 has brought the increased burden of sickness, anxiety, fear, discouragement, mental health problems, and many other social disruptions. How do we make sense of all this?

Reinvent and Reroute

The life and behavior of *Safari ants* is an example of reinventing and rerouting. Under the shock of disruption on their journey by humans or animals through fire raid, human feet, or other means, the ants have a way of regrouping, and designing new paths for their onward journeys. From a bird's eye views, when the ants are disrupted, they seem lost, disoriented, and destined to lonely and death-ward wanderings. Yet, after some little wandering from the initial shock, safari ants often regroup and reorganize their journeys effectively. This seems to be what the world must do - regrouping from the shock of Covid-19, and recreate their destination. With Corona virus, however, finding bearing is more complex in the light of the effects it has had on individuals, families, organizations and nations. It does not satisfy to keep the 'new normal' if it implies evading Covid-19, sickness, anxiety, fear, hunger, and so on. We must seek and hope for a new normal in which there is livelihood, predictability, safety, and prosperity. Even with the WHO warning that Covid-19 pandemic might turn into an endemic, there must be hopes for a decisive victory over the virus, and its impact.

For a fact individuals and entities have experienced significant turbulence, and being on the edge. For organizations, reinventing and re-routing implies designing *business continuity plans* and exploring *sustainability* as priority. An organization like the Fellowship of Christian Unions (FOCUS) Kenya, needed to quickly reflect on the worth and relevance of its mission, in a suddenly new operating environment. Recognizing that every corner of the world is shaken and grappling with similar questions and issues, it was important to designing a *ministry continuity plan,* and sustainability that focuses on the mission of the organization and within the core values. It means that regrouping did not just mean survival, but regrouping move forward in the direction of its mission. For example, the immediate response to write a Bible study guide, *Walking in the Shadow of Death*, was within our mission, but also a relevant response to the question, "Why Corona Virus?" Volatility and uncertainty can so easily displace the mission of an organization and its core values in efforts to survive the times. Reinventing is therefore not merely seeking survival, and rerouting does not imply a different destination or drift from original mission. The action by FOCUS to move scripture engagement onto the digital platform was create a new route for the mission - ensuring that the key stakeholders, particularly the university Christian students, remain engaged within the vision.   Yet, even in re-routing, the organization's core values were carried along to inform identity and operations. So, that even in crisis times, FOCUS values of *Integrity, excellence, student-centeredness, Scripture engagement,* and *team work* needed to breathe life in the reinvention and re-routing. However, everybody may have realized that re-inventing and rerouting with a pandemic like Covid-19 will be a longer journey that requires both grace and courage.

Grace to adapt and courage to act

If you do not know how it feels or looks like, you will neither find it nor see it!

For its negative impact, Covid-19 provides us with multiple hostile curves to flatten other than the disease itself. For example, on a global scale, many people have lost their loved ones to death, living behind a trail of sorrow, economic lack, and general disorientation. Within a pandemic situation like COVID-19 this refreshes the old questions in a resounding manner -the questions about the existence, presence, and character of God. While non-believers begin to embrace the possibility of a creator-being, some believers begin to doubt the novel attributes of God. Is he still loving and powerful? Is he relevant? Can there be hope in such a God? Sometimes God allows persons, organizations, and nations to experience difficult and painful moments in life. In his sovereign will, he allows or even causes people to go face the mountain rather than the getting around it or over it! It has been one way of the divine calling for our collective attention towards Him. Isn't it worth it when everyone is forced to ask the question of the purpose of their existence on earth, and to begin to face the direction of the earth's maker for rescue?

In the book of Numbers chapter 21, there is a story of Israel in which God punishes Israel for their incessant rebellion. The plague of snakes ensnares Israel and it leads to untold deaths as a result of bites from the venomous snakes. However, in their desperation and when Moses offers prayers of mercy, God heeds to their cries. God instructs that Moses makes a bronze serpent and hang it on a tree, so that every Israelite who is bitten and looks at the bronze snake survives the effect of the snake bites. The experience of Israel points to the depth of hopelessness that can characterize human beings in times of crises, and God in a gracious way stepping in to rescue.

In the case of Covid-19, first, people's attention has been drawn to God for hope and miraculous healing and recovery from effects of the pandemic. Every single release of a Covid-19 patience inspires hope to the communities and nations. In the hospital beds, quarantine centers, and policy-making rooms, God is healing, comforting, and guiding in his wisdom. In the laboratories, the scientists can hope in God's guidance as they seek to find a vaccine; the political leaders can seek his wisdom in making decisions to mitigate the spread, treatment, and other effects of covid-19. God himself created the universe, and therefore he cannot fail in his will at anything. More importantly, just like in the dessert journeys of Israel, God has made *provisions*. For believers and humanity, God is the source of all knowledge, all power, and all wisdom. We may and must try all the good things possible to reverse the losses, but we must rely on him as the ultimate healer, provider, and one who has the destiny of the world in his hands.

Since Covid-19 pandemic emerged, in the religious cycle the question has been – is God punishing the world? This not-withstanding, the need for divine intervention has been widely echoed. There is no manifest time when God's silence appears louder than in crisis times. Even when we call him instinctively for help, we often settle with the feeling that he has abandoned us. Yet the world leaders have publicly gravitated towards divine help beyond the actions in the scientific laboratories, the organization of health infrastructure, and the boardroom strategies to manage the spread and effects of Corona virus.

Second, individuals and communities need the grace to *accept* a covid-19 situation, especially when there is evidence of surging numbers of those infected in the pandemic, and the attendant chaos it brings. Like in the case of Israel when the snakes never stopped biting, Covid-19 situation may persist, but God is attending. Often, when people are in a drifting boat in stormy waters, they always keep hoping that even if the boat lands in an expected shore, it would still dock safely. A story is told of king David (2 Samuel 12), a man whose life had many twists and turns even as he led the nation of Israel. In one instance he sinned against God by succumbing to his passions that led him to sexual sin, and consequently to murder. Out of the sexual sin was born a child whom David embraced. However, the Bible says that the Lord struck the child with illness, presumably as a punishment against David. While the child was sick, David displayed signs of a very distressed person. He fasted, he lay in sackcloth, and pleaded with God to spare the child. So desperate did David appear that when the child died, the servants were too afraid to report just in case David reacted outrageously. However, on hearing the news of the death of the child, David refreshed himself and got into a feasting mode. When the perplexed servants inquired why David was behaving in a manner they had not expected, David replied, *"While the child was still alive, I fasted and wept. I thought, 'Who knows? The LORD may be gracious to me and let the child live.' But now that he is dead, why should I go on fasting? Can I bring him back again? I will go to him, but he will not return to me."* (2 Sam 12:22-23).

While the story of David in this instance is not prescriptive of exactly how we ought to respond to disaster, we see an example of a leader who had grace to accept the uncomfortable realities, and begin to adapt and move on. Although the subsequent narrative tells of the messy consequences occasioned by David's sin, David still had hope in God, not only for his personal redemption, but for his leadership. David's rulership depicts the nature of a fallen world in which many things go wrong, yet God remains the hope that steers the world that he created.

In God, we can find the strength to *adapt* to a new reality in a new 'bad' normal. We can also gain the courage to *act* towards a promising reality in the circumstances. The bible says that David *"comforted his wife Bathsheba", and moved on with his life* (v. 24). By means of prayer, there can be grace to reinvent and improve the lot before us. Nations can have their economies revived, and it is only through God's lenses that one can be able to see beyond the horizon, and explore afresh. God can also grant a new bearing when livelihood means is lost. In the days of Elijah, when he had to self-quarantine for his safety, the Lord caused the ravens to bring him bread and meat. The Lord also provided a brook from which to quench Elijah's thirst (1Ki 17:4-6 NIV). In an uneven world, where some people can be sick for lack of food while other are sick for too much of food, God still remains the provider for the hungry. We may miss the *starters* and *desserts*, but God can use 'ravens' to supply needs. Christians should pray that God provides through ravens. But they should also pray that they become the very ravens God will use.

Third, during this pandemic, people have had to reflect on their beliefs and life philosophies. Christians have questioned their faith, wondering whether they can trust the God they believe, in the light of the suffering Corona virus has exposed the world to. These are historical reflections that have only been revived by the pandemic. How can God be so good and so powerful in the circumstances? Could he have caused this, and to what end? There are biblical models of what it means to have hope even in bad and confusing times. Many biblical heroes upheld their faith and trust in God because they remembered his steadfast love, faithfulness, and power in their lives and leadership. Job, for example, when faced with the dilemma of his suffering, chose to cling to God irrespective of the rational arguments before him. Even though he understood that God had afflicted him (Job 30:11), he says *"Though he slay me, yet will I hope in him..."* (Job 13:15a NIV).

It is instructive that pandemics have happened before, and even when God allowed some like the *Spanish flu* to have three waves in its resurgence, he still held his world in his hands. Understanding that we are in fallen world, that nothing happens without God's knowledge, and that some ultimate suffering can lead to eternity with God. On many fronts the virus has exposed the underlying ills in our societies. Throughout the world, the virus unveiled further the uneven global economic divides. It has also shown the limitations of human leadership when the world is struck. Even expert medical views on the pandemic have been in discordance with each other, creating further confused into an already anxious situation. Individual rights verses sacrifice for common good has characterized spending, and church leaders and prophets have disagreed on their interpretation of the happenings. At the end of the day, God is his wisdom remains the hope, for he was before all things, and in his son "all things hold together" (Col 1:16-17 NIV).

Fourthly, out of the pandemic people will yearn for good news. Whereas, it is ultimate for people to be reconciled to God, this good news should evident in addressing the needs of communities and nations. The vision of Jesus is well articulated in Luke 4:16-18:

> *"The Spirit of the Lord is on me, because he has anointed me to proclaim good news to the poor. He has sent me to proclaim freedom for the prisoners and recovery of sight for the blind, to set the oppressed free, to proclaim the year of the Lord's favor" (Luke 4:18-19 NIV).*

In this vision, the gospel is good news in all dimensions for God's people – God's people are not only those who believe in Him. God gives hope to all –all humanity. Good news speaks to the sinners, the hungry, the mentality ill, and addicts of all kinds. This is the picture of hope that Jesus' mission depicts, and the world longs for during and after the pandemic. The church ought to lead in this hope that is holistic in its approach.

God's sovereignty over all

When life is experienced through the eyes of history and in hindsight, things are clearer and solutions are easy to imagine. But when you are experiencing a live pandemic, when you are in the middle of the very storm, and when the storm appears to only get worse, it can feel like eternity, and confusion can reign supreme. There can be immense challenges, where fear is pulpable, and suffering overwhelming. Sometimes in the shock of suffering, our faith may seem too diminished to begin to be hopeful. Yet these are always the true moments to seek hope, and help others find hope in God. God's power does not need the requisite of human abilities. God is sovereign, complete, and able, and every small step of faith meets his full grace.

Lastly, this pandemic has put a spotlight on leaders than ever before. Uncertainty of the moment compels people to be more demanding, more in need of clearer leadership. When people are led, they often trust and place their hopes in their leaders. Yet quite often even leaders try to inspire confidence even when they are not sure where they are leading towards. Pandemics make leaders vulnerable to guess work. Yet for the sake of his people, God's grace is available to guides leadership. King David of Israel demonstrates that despite the perception of having enough manpower, arsenals, and a good record of success, he needed to enquire from the Lord not only what battles to fight (2 Sam 5:19; 1 Chronicles 14:10), but also how to fight the battles (2 Sam 5:23; 1 Chronicles 14:14). The call to pray for leadership in a pandemic and crises situation is always urgent. For in his mercy and compassion, God can override the actions of leadership and move events in history for his purposes. God can still move leaders in the right redemptive directions to save the world from self-destruction. He has power over all prevailing forces. God is a trusted ally in doing good!

Therefore, only a sovereign God, the creator, can be the true refuge, source of comfort, and provider. His redemption is not only for this life, but also the life to come. To know God is to come to terms with where true hope resides. At the height of this pandemic, the need for Jesus is a constant. His invitation is also sure and resounding in love. Our need for hope and rest has already been supplied. This is our hope! Jesus says,"

> *Come to me, all you who are weary and burdened, and I will give you rest. Take my yoke upon you and learn from me, for I am gentle and humble in heart, and you will find rest for your souls. For my yoke is easy and my burden is light"* (Mat 11:28-30 NIV).